The Unabridged Woman

The Unabridged Woman

A Guide to Growing Up Female

Bobbie McKay, Ph.D.

The Pilgrim Press
New York City

Library of Congress Cataloging in Publication Data

McKay, Bobbie, 1931-
    The unabridged woman.

    1. Women—Psychology.   I.   Title.
HQ1206.M323   301.41'2   79-14297
ISBN 0-8298-0369-6

The Pilgrim Press   132 West 31 Street
New York, New York 10001

*This book is dedicated to the
women and men of the Glenview
Community Church and Nursery
School, who shared their lives
with me, who let me love them,
and who loved and taught me in
the process;
to my children, who first showed
me about loving and touching,
who shared my struggle to grow,
and who understood what I had to
do;
to my husband, who has nurtured
and loved me, and who has been
fiercely partisan in my journey to
become unabridged and free.*

Contents

CHAPTER 1
A Starting Place

We used to think we knew all there was to know about growth and development. We were pretty well convinced adulthood began at twenty-one, and that, in the years between zero and twenty-one, we automatically learned all there was to know about being grown up.

But we're finally discovering that growth and change continue throughout life. It's not as if we magically reach a time when we're all grown up, or live happily ever after, or behave in a mature, adult fashion. We've discovered that growth and change are a *process,* a kind of "becoming" in which we continually unfold, becoming more open to our individual selves as well as to the world around us.

In some ways it was easier being a woman fifty years ago. One knew exactly what the course of one's life would be, and with rare exceptions, women followed traditional roles that were well defined and quite secure.

It was even easier being a woman in the 1960s, during the height of the women's liberation movement, when everyone made a concerted effort to challenge traditional ways of living. But I believe that women today have a more difficult situation to deal with and are asking a different kind of question: What shall I be liberated *toward,* rather than what shall I be liberated *from?* The issues of growth and change, the issues of what directions we should choose in our lives are the most crucial ones we face.

1

We know that, as human beings, we're constantly pushed to grow by an inner urgency that doesn't cease unless we consciously turn it off.

But we're not really sure who we want to be, and we have trouble going with the tide of growth and change. We may know we've been "liberated," but, like children in a toy store, where all kinds of choices are open to us, we're nearly driven crazy by our anxiety to make the *right* choice. In this process of being liberated toward, rather than liberated from, we discover what we're really being liberated toward is a new way of being: a new way of learning and growing, a new way of sharing and loving. Liberation toward, rather than from, focuses our attention on the *process* of growth and change, rather than on the product or end result. Liberation toward, rather than from, means being liberated toward the marvelous possibility of growth and change in our lives. And liberation toward, rather than from, *always* includes our relationships with significant other persons in our lives.

As human beings, we're constantly confronted with the possibility of growth and change. Indeed, if we don't continue to grow we usually feel unhappy, frustrated, resentful, angry, helpless, or hopeless. We become more rigid, more defensive, and more isolated from the world around us.

Yet, sometimes we find it difficult to acknowledge we must continue to *work* at the process of growth and change all our lives. It's never over and done with, and it's rarely accomplished without significant work on our part. Life doesn't allow us to sit back, relax, and pronounce that we're finished products.

Once we accept the ongoing sense of process we find life seems to exist as a series of growth or change experiences that can be readily identified by their component parts.

Change always begins with a sense of uneasiness or discomfort that signals things aren't the way they should be. And it's almost always followed by a strong sense of *resistance* to the whole process. We may try to deny there's any need to change via a variety of devices used to con ourselves into maintaining the status quo. We may set up further resistances by feeling fearful, guilty, or by questioning if we really *want* to change.

But once into the process and past some of the resistances, we find that change and growth mean discovering more and more about ourselves. Change and growth mean opening up our capacity for self-expression. And change and growth always include the possibility of deeper and more significant relationships with those around us. Simply stated, our personal liberation begins with us, with our process of becoming, growing, changing. *But it must move us toward others in order for the process to be complete.*

In understanding ourselves it's imperative that we include an understanding of ourselves in the relationships we hold or have held. For it's out of these relationships that we can better gain an understanding of who we are and what we choose to be.

As a psychologist and an ordained minister, I've worked with a variety of groups of women: women of all ages; women at various places in their process of growth and development. Their struggles to grow have been the focus for this book. In our times together we have always begun with the immediate issues of children, marriage, in-laws, careers; but we have always found ourselves moving into the deeper issues of self: self-worth, self-understanding, self-concern; recognition of the deeper feelings of pain and anger that we all carry with us. And we have learned that within the context of a *caring relationship* the possibility for growth and change is immeasurably enhanced, whether in a group situation or in a one-to-one, person-to-person experience. In fact, the simple act of caring and being concerned is the most profound agent of healing that we know.

The quotations that appear in this book are from women and men in individual psychotherapy, or from persons in groups with which I have worked. They have shared themselves and their stories that others might be helped in their own "journeys toward growth."

It's not easy, this business of being liberated and free. For it removes all the old resistances to change we formerly relied on, and it forces us into an awful awareness that, whether we choose to grow or choose not to grow, *the choice we make is ours alone.*

The Unabridged Woman discusses the stages in the struggle toward growth and is written for all who choose to be unabridged and free. It begins with the assurance that our *obligation* is to grow . . . to dream . . . to create . . . and *to come alive!*

CHAPTER 2

Women and Their Feelings:
The Beginning of Growth

G rowth always begins at the place where we are—with our *feelings*, whatever they might be.

The women who come to see me individually, or collectively in groups, feel varying degrees of pain and frustration. They may be anxious, confused, guarded, sad, angry, or resentful. But they have one thing in common: they'd expected one thing from life and were finding life was offering them something quite different from what they'd anticipated. They were feeling disappointed and unhappy. What they'd been led to believe would happen, when adulthood finally arrived, was simply not happening to them. They'd been duped by a middle-class myth about adulthood that goes something like this: When you get a job, get married, have a child, and buy a home, everything will be OK.

> *I'd expected that when I got married, everything would be all right. I was sure my husband and I could handle anything that came along. What a bad deal to find out that being married was just like being at home—except that now I'm doing all the work.*
>
> ≈

*All I ever wanted to do was to get married and have babies.
No one ever told me I might have a child who had temper
tantrums in every store we ever went to or who would drive
me up a wall until I wished I never had a child.*

≈

*I always thought that being a suburban housewife would
mean lots of neighbors to be with . . . but my neighbors
don't even know I exist. Most of them don't even say hello.
I really feel all alone most of the time.*

≈

*I'm so lonely I find myself fantasizing all the time . . .
sometimes I'm not sure where fantasy ends and reality
begins.*

The toughest part for these women was actually to let the world
know they were suffering. In fact, they'd already spent a great deal
of time not only denying their own unhappiness, but also trying to
place the blame for their unhappiness on someone or something
else. Most of us, when confronted with an onslaught of unwanted
or painful feelings, will do anything to get rid of them.

It's a fact that restlessness—a sense of something being wrong—
always heralds the first stage of growth. We don't grow when
everything goes smoothly. There's no reason to. But a feeling of
disappointment, a sense that things aren't right, always indicates a
need for change. Although we may admit this need for change, we
almost always slow down the process by first *denying* the existence
of such feelings or by *externalizing or projecting* them.

Denial goes something like this:

*Well, things aren't really so bad. They could be a lot worse.
After all, my husband's a good provider.*

≈

At least we have good neighbors and a nice home.

≈

*How can I complain when I see people around me with so
much less than I have, and they're not complaining?*

≈

*At least my kids are going to have the kind of life I never had.
I don't mind being without. That's what being a parent is all
about.*

In this case, we try to turn off our pain and disappointment by being altruistic about the rest of the world. After all, how can we complain when we're not suffering or starving, like so much of the rest of the world?

Externalizing feelings goes like this:

If it weren't for my husband's job, everything would be OK.

~

If it weren't for my mother-in-law, my husband and I would get along fine.

≈

Our family would be just fine if we could get rid of our teenagers.

≈

If I could just lose ten pounds, I'm sure I'd feel a lot better about myself.

≈

If I had a bigger house, I wouldn't have so much junk around.

You can recognize externalization because it always involves something or someone else. That's the way we get the heat off of us. If *someone* or *something* else would do something differently, then *we'd* feel better. It looks great in print, but it's not likely to produce better feelings for us. Anytime we're dependent on someone or something else to give us good feelings, we're asking to be disappointed. Externalization says it's not really *my fault* that I feel unhappy, depressed, or angry. It's really caused by something or someone else, so I don't have to take responsibility for the way I feel.

Finally, as a form of denying our feelings, we might try *projecting them* onto someone else. Projecting is a good psychological word that deals with ascribing our *own* feelings to *others*. That way, we don't have to feel the feelings but can continue to deny their existence. Anger is a feeling that we often project onto others. We do this because anger is an emotion we don't feel comfortable with. Women, in particular, have a hard time expressing their anger.

Society has recognized anger as being unfeminine, an emotion that men could feel but nice girls couldn't. And so the idealized images that women have held about themselves rarely included being open and honest with their own anger or rage, but rather encouraged projections and denial of such feelings.

Consequently, women will often raise the question: Are you angry with me? When, in fact, what they really mean is: I'm angry with you, but I'm afraid to tell you.

Other projections go like this:

You *seem so cold and unconcerned.* [*Translate that to:* I am feeling cold and uncaring but that doesn't fit into the way I should be feeling.]

≈

Your mother (brother, father, etc.) doesn't seem to like me. [*Meaning:* I'm not able to recognize my own feelings of discomfort about them.]

≈

I can't imagine why you're angry. What do you have to be angry about? [*The implication is that:* I have a lot to feel angry about, but at least I'm holding it in and not expressing it. The only avenue of expression for anger that I have is through projecting it onto you. But then I can feel frustrated with you for being able to express the anger that I can't own in myself.]

≈

Why do you always treat me like an inadequate child, incapable of any decision? [*Which means:* I feel like an inadequate child most of the time, and I am angry with myself. But I can't stand those feelings and will project them onto you, calling them your attitude toward me. Then I'll feel justified in becoming angry with you for treating me that way.]

Projection, like externalization, takes the blame off of us and places our own feelings of anger, inadequacy, and pain on someone else. Yet, ultimately, projection works no better than externalization; it only postpones the painful moment when we must take credit and responsibility for our own feelings.

If the first stage in growth is admitting that all is not well in our individual situations, then the second stage consists of owning our own feelings: which is to say, not denying, externalizing, or projecting our feelings, but recognizing they exist *within us.* This is particularly hard for us, as women, to do, because we've been programmed in a unique way—programmed to be "nice," I call it. Most of us have a highly developed "nice" side, a side that gives us permission to express our "nice" emotions. But we have a poorly developed, though nonetheless active, "not-so-nice" side. We know the feelings we're *supposed* to have.

> *I know I should feel happy. I've got a good husband, two nice kids, a couple of cars, and a beautiful home. But I'm really depressed, and I don't ever feel very happy about anything. I don't understand what's wrong.*
>
> ≈
>
> *I know I should be grateful for what I've got. My husband is kind: he never gives me a hard time. He's always understanding. But his kindness is driving me crazy.*

What we're unprepared for is the way we *actually feel* some of the time.

> *I never knew what a bitch I was until I got married.*
>
> ≈
>
> *I never dreamed I'd scream at my kids, but now I know how parents feel who abuse their children. Sometimes I've wanted to pick them up and throw them across the room.*
>
> ≈
>
> *I always thought I was a pretty nice person, until I found myself out of control, screaming at my husband. I still don't know what set me off, but it was awful. I'd never done that before.*

Because females have been traditionally called "the more emotional sex," most people believe women are comfortable openly expressing their feelings. What's not mentioned, however, is that women are encouraged to limit themselves to certain emotions. It's permissible to feel sad, tired, depressed, anxious, unhappy, teary, dependent, and inadequate. It's not as acceptable to feel rage, fury, anger, and resentment, let alone express such feelings.

What emerges repeatedly from women who seek counseling help is that they've tried to be nice, to do the right thing. They've tried

9

the power of positive thinking and the power of positive action. As one woman put it:

> I even prayed every day to get rid of my angry feelings. I read every book I could find on being a good Christian. But I'm still angry all the time. And I feel so resentful toward my husband and my children; I think constantly of what it might feel like to leave them and go far away. I really don't like them much of the time, and I hate myself for feeling that way.

These are some of the unacceptable feelings we're not supposed to have.

But feelings are real, and what's continually apparent is that the more we try to hide or run away from them, the more likely they are to accumulate inside us. It's like filling a garbage can with all our unexpressed feelings. We've been programmed to express the "nice" feelings and have been advised to throw out the "not-so-nice" ones. And we tell ourselves that the consequences of expressing the "bad" feelings would be catastrophic for us.

> If my husband ever knew some of the things I fantasize about, he'd divorce me.
>
> ≈
>
> If I ever let my neighbors know how I really feel about them, they'd never speak to me again.
>
> ≈
>
> If I ever told my mother how angry she makes me, she'd never forgive me.

If we keep stuffing away our anger, our disappointment, our frustration, our fears, there'll come a day when we can't pack them away anymore, for the garbage can will have overflowed.

> I don't know what happened. It just seemed to take over. But all the weeks and months and years of frustration finally erupted, and I dredged up every rotten thing he ever did. He told me I was simply being emotional, and that made me so angry I started hitting him.

Or perhaps, unconsciously, we'll begin to express our anger and resentment through such physical symptoms as ulcers, colitis, backaches, headaches, or premenstrual tension. We call this somatization, a condition in which the body expresses for us those feelings that are unacceptable to us. If we can't verbally own our pain and anger, then our symptoms will speak for us. Feelings will ultimately have their expression, if not through verbalizations, then through our body language or through some physical symptom.

Maybe we'll find ourselves in what's called a neurotic depression, with all the anger and rage we feel turned back in on ourselves and experienced as "the blues," helplessness, and hopelessness.

Many women find themselves unable to cope with the demands of life, especially as they include making changes and choices that are self-motivated and independent. Rather than take responsibility for our own lives, rather than make demands on those around us to make life better, we feel helpless and hopeless to change anything. Our disappointment and anger toward others is unacceptable. Our disappointment and anger in ourselves is enormous. Therefore, our only recourse in a depressed state is to tune out the world; to move inside ourselves; to feel bad about who we are; to feel angry and frustrated that we can't behave differently; perhaps to withdraw completely. Some women in a depressed state simply go to bed and try to suppress all their feelings. A neurotic depression is a closed system in which we operate only with ourselves, eliminating the rest of the world.

Or we might try to channel all that neurotic energy and turn it into what psychologists call a reaction formation. We take all the bad stuff and turn it into good stuff, and become supermothers and superwives: perfect moms who fall apart when children are no longer at home to need them; or perfect wives who cannot understand it when their husbands leave them for other women after thirty years of seemingly perfect marriage. Those who must use reaction formation to deny their feelings become superworkaholics who continually do for others in order to make sure that no one in the world (themselves included) has any awareness of some of the "bad" feelings they might have. Cloaked in good works, they cannot understand it when their kids are unappreciative or their husbands driven away by their incessant doing for them. Supermoms cannot allow themselves to feel the normal range of feelings that all people feel in the relationships they hold. Consequently, they must convert such feelings into acceptable form, frequently expressed by multitudinous good works and deep self-denial.

Perhaps we make a different kind of adjustment and become afternoon drunks . . . or successful suicides.

Whatever we do, our feelings won't disappear. They'll express themselves one way or another.

So how does growth begin? It begins, tentatively at first, as an open acknowledgment of what we *feel*. For the real issue resides within us, not in the external persons or events of our lives. The more we deny, or externalize, or project our feelings, the more likely they are to accumulate and explode. The more we tell ourselves:

Well, there's no reason to feel that way, or:

I've really nothing to complain about, or:

What's wrong with me that I have those feelings when

nobody else seems to . . .

the more likely we are to feel more resentment and anger than ever.

In every human being, and in every human relationship, there exists a full spectrum of feelings. When we allow ourselves to be human, when we can risk sharing our total humanness, we've made the first steps toward growth.

One of the "miracles" that occurs when women gather in groups, or when they enter into a counseling relationship, is that they discover two highly significant facts:

1. It's really OK to feel angry and resentful toward your husband, your children, your neighbors, and your friends, as well as warm and loving.
2. Everyone else has had the same feelings but has hesitated to express them to anyone.

And perhaps even more significantly, once these tentative feelings have been explored, the real issues begin to emerge:

I've known I felt disappointed in my husband for a long time. What I'm beginning to become aware of is that I'm

12

really disappointed in myself *and the mess I've made of my own life. That's where the real hurt lies.*

≈

I've been blaming my mother for most of my problems. If she'd been more loving, I'd have made a better life for myself. Maybe that's true. But it doesn't do me any good anymore to blame her. There are things I want for myself, and blaming her won't help me get them.

≈

I've been furious with my children and almost uncontrollable sometimes in my anger. I know if I were honest with myself, I'd own up to feeling frightened about being a mother. I want to be a good mother, and I don't want to mess up my kids. But I'm scared that I'm going to ruin them, and the more scared I become, the more angry I get.

≈

Sometimes I get awfully angry and resentful toward my friends and neighbors. They always seem to be doing things for one another, but no one ever does anything for me. I know I'm feeling rejected and unloved, but I'm afraid to tell anyone else how I feel. So I just get mad, and I guess I must look mad . . . so I don't get anywhere at all.

We're born, each of us, as loving beings. We get frustrated when we can't get what we want and need. We grow up telling ourselves it really doesn't matter after all.

But we continue, beneath our paper-thin mask of bravado, to need to be accepted, cared about, and cared for, as well as to care about and to care for others. We continue to feel frustrated and unhappy when we feel rejected and unloved. We respond with equal rejection and unloving behavior toward those who seem to frustrate us. And we continue to kid ourselves that it really doesn't matter.

Yet, it *does* matter, and the path toward growth reminds us of two important facts:

1. We do want and need to be loved, appreciated, cared about, and respected all the days of our lives.

2. We do get angry and frustrated and resentful when our needs for love, respect, recognition, and care are *not* met.

Our needs for love and respect, care and concern have been with us since birth. Without sufficient warmth, nurturing, and care we would not have survived as infants. For years we were totally dependent on others to provide for these needs of love and protection. One of the frustrations we have as children is this very posture of dependency that makes us so vulnerable to the whims of the adults who care for us and that causes us so much fear and rage when we feel unloved or unwanted.

The important difference between us as children and us as adults is that we can both acknowledge our need *and* do something about getting our needs met when reaching adulthood. As children, we could only *hope* someone would respond to our needs. As adults, we have new options and much more power.

We have the capacity to meet our own needs and to produce our own satisfactions, in a way we never had before. One of the most significant advantages of adulthood is our potential for personal power, the ability to get what we need to live fuller, richer lives.

Growth begins with an acknowledgment that all is not well all the time; that there are areas of dissatisfaction that need improvement; and that we must be as honest as possible in describing our dissatisfactions. Only as we come to terms with what we *don't* want or *don't* have can we expect to get what we *do* want and *must* have out of life.

Growth begins, as does all of life, by confronting trust. Can I trust me? Can I trust you? Can I tell you what I need? Can I begin to get what I want?

As one patient shared with me:

The hardest thing in the world for me to do is tell you I need you. I'm so afraid to be needy. I'm so afraid you'll take advantage of my need. It's very difficult to trust that you won't hurt me.

So it is with all of us . . . at the beginning of growth.

CHAPTER 3

Resistances to Growth

You can always tell you're growing by your *resistance* to the process. It's a sure sign growth is taking place. As human beings, we have a unique capacity to struggle *against* that which is most likely to benefit us.

As mentioned earlier, once we begin to be aware of our feelings, we usually try, initially, to deny them or transfer them to someone else. But once we've owned them and accepted the fact that they're ours, Stage II in the growth process begins. Psychologists call this stage "resistance," and it means we put up one helluva struggle to avoid getting better.

One of the first resistances we erect has to do with our *right* to get something for ourselves. It's called "being selfish." Whenever I speak to women's groups about getting something for themselves, there's an immediate reaction that says: to get anything for oneself is to be *selfish*.

> *I just couldn't do that. Why, that would be terribly selfish. I just don't understand why you'd even suggest such a thing. I have to be responsible for my husband and children first. I just can't go about doing my own thing, without regard for the feelings of others.*

≈

15

I think it would simply be terrible if everyone just did what they wanted to do. That would be very irresponsible. I think it's unchristian.

Among churchwomen, in particular, there's a persistent belief that being "selfish" is antithetical to being Christian. The truly good Christian woman is seen as an all-giving, all-loving individual who pays no attention to her own needs and cares only about the concerns of others. (I'm not sure where this notion came from, but Jesus certainly didn't advocate it.) However, it's a myth that's persisted through the years, and when I try to challenge that myth, I'm usually greeted with shock and resistance.

But the plain truth is, unless you get something for yourself, you simply can't give anything to anyone else. You may delude yourself that you are, and you may be able to fool yourself and others for a long time, but eventually you'll run dry. It's like pouring from a pitcher: you can only pour the contents of the pitcher. Then you have to fill it up with something in order to continue to pour something.

People who continually give sometimes operate from a position of feeling inadequate or unworthy.

If I give a lot to others, perhaps they'll like me.

$\approx$

If I give a lot to others, perhaps eventually I'll get something back for me.

They may also operate from a need to control.

If I keep giving you things, you'll be in debt to me, and I can control the amount of indebtedness by how much I give you.

People who give a lot frequently meet people who take a lot, and then the givers feel more frustrated than ever because the takers want and expect more and more and seldom give back to the givers. We often see this phenomenon in dysfunctional family relationships. Mother is usually the complainer.

16

I simply don't know what's the matter. I've been a devoted mother. I'm always home. I try to do everything I can to make life easier for the family. I don't make any demands on anyone. I never complain. For years I've driven the kids everywhere, anytime they wanted. But . . . no one ever does anything to help me. And when I ask the kids to pick up their clothes or to clean their rooms, they get angry or just ignore me. I guess that's the worst of it. I'm just ignored all the time.

And that's quite true. Once takers know there's a giver around, they're more than willing to let the givers give. It's a depressing situation for the woman who has genuinely given throughout the years to discover there are few rewards in it for her. She's like an orange that's been squeezed to death. She's dried out and unattractive and there's nothing left in her to give.

But it's an exceedingly hard pattern for most women to give up, for two reasons:

1. On paper, it looks good. To be a warm, loving, giving person, who makes life easy for those around her, is a very appealing picture.
2. It's the feminine stereotype most of us grew up with, and therefore it's been reinforced by the culture in which we live.

The problem is, we go about the whole thing backwards. To be a warm, loving, exciting person is perfectly admirable. The fault lies in our approach. For we can't be warm, loving, and exciting without feeling that way ourselves, and we can't feel that way if we're constantly denying our emotions and our own needs for warmth and love.

To begin to be selfish, which means to be self-concerned, is to begin to build deep reservoirs within from which we can draw when we choose to be warm and giving. When we take the time to give to ourselves; when we actually do something for ourselves that makes us feel good; when we engage in any activity that allows us to be expressive of who we are, then the quality of our relationships with others changes remarkably.

I've always wanted to paint. And one day I actually got the courage to paint something on the basement walls. I figured even if it was lousy, no one would mind it down there, and I could always cover it up with more paint if I really couldn't stand it. But I felt absolutely marvelous doing it. It was something I did. I couldn't believe it. And you know, my husband's proud of it; he takes everyone downstairs to see it.

≈

I've always hated winter. I get depressed every year with the constant staying in with the kids: the unending colds, the grayness, the lack of warmth. One day I got tired of the whole thing. I turned up the heat, got out our shorts, made iced tea and potato salad, cooked hot dogs in the fireplace, and just pretended that summer was back. It changed our whole family. We still talk about the day mother changed the seasons. I feel good about it.

You don't have to go out and get a job to be self-concerned (although you might want to). You don't have to be a creative, artistic person in the usual sense of painting, composing, or writing (although you may choose to). You don't have to do anything drastic or bizarre. But you *do* need to change your focus from *without* to *within*.

Whenever you meet your own needs, whenever you give something to yourself, you're in a much better position to give to others.

I find that on those mornings when I wake up grumpy and ugly, my anger and resentment mount at an ever-increasing rate until I explode, unless I take at least ten to fifteen minutes for myself alone. Sometimes I just stick the kids in front of the television set and go up and take a bath and get dressed in something that makes me feel worthwhile, instead of like a frumpy housewife. Sometimes I try meditating. Mostly I find that when I feel pressed upon, I have to stop and give myself something before I can give anything to anyone else, except my anger or resentment.

I'd like to banish the word selfish forever and substitute the term self-concerned. To be self-concerned means to have self-respect. And to have self-respect always invites the respect of others.

The more I ran around doing everything for the family, the more they expected me to be available and ready to do anything at anytime. I resented being the chief chauffeur, cook, and cleaner. But when I decided to go back to school and was simply not able to do all the things I used to, I found that everyone pitched in, and to my amazement, all those things that everyone couldn't do when I was available suddenly became quite easy to do. And I found my kids were telling their friends all about the fact that their mom was back in college. I know they feel good about what I'm doing, and they've proven to themselves that they can do a lot of things they never thought they could.

And finally, to be self-concerned is to provide an excellent model for all around you of what being an adult is all about.

I don't want my kids to grow up feeling like they have to do all the things I tell myself I have to do. I'd much rather they develop themselves as persons. I want them to grow up and really feel good about themselves.

The way to teach that lesson is to do it yourself. We learn best by example.

Being self-concerned is a process of learning to listen to what's going on inside you. It's to hear your dreams, your desires, your hopes, your wants. But it requires listening without judgment or criticism. All too often we're too quick to judge our dreams as being unattainable.

I've always wanted to take dancing lessons. But that seems really stupid. I mean, it's just too expensive and the family can't spend that kind of money on dancing lessons for me.

≈

I'd like to work full time, but that would mean I wouldn't be home after school when the kids get home. I'm afraid of what the neighbors would say about my kids being home alone. I just can't do that.

This brings us directly to our second big resistance to change: fear. Once a woman is convinced that perhaps she might listen to her inner voice, her usual response to her inner voice's message is to feel afraid.

I'd be too afraid to do that. I mean, what would everyone think? I just couldn't do it.

≈

I've never done anything like that. I wouldn't know how to begin. I'd be afraid I'd botch it.

≈

I'm afraid to find out I can't do what I've been dreaming about. As long as it's an untested dream, then I don't have to face the fact I might not be able to.

Right away, the whole fear sequence is aroused. I'd like to, but I'm afraid to, therefore I can't. Overcoming fear is an exceedingly satisfactory experience.

I'd always been afraid to drive to Chicago. There were so many things I wanted to see, but I just couldn't get up the courage to drive it alone. When I finally couldn't stand it any longer, I forced myself to try. It was the most marvelous day I've had in a long, long time.

≈

I'd always wanted to sing in the church choir, but for some reason I'd been scared about it. I practically had anxiety attacks each time I had to walk down the center aisle at church. But gradually, I've gotten over my fear, and it feels good to finally be able to do something I have wanted to do.

Fear is subtle and difficult to work with. For we're afraid not only of our own incapacity to do something, but also of what others might think of us. Sometimes we even fear we might be successful at something and that would really change us.

I'd like to be a doctor, and I frankly believe I could make it in medical school. But I'm afraid of the cost to my husband and children. I know I'd enjoy myself so much I wouldn't be home very much. I'm almost afraid I'd find out I was much happier being a doctor than a wife and a mother.

Fear, as a resistance to growth and change, gets more complicated as it involves the feelings and attitudes of others.

I'm afraid it would hurt my husband if I went back to work.
He tries to be a good provider, and if I start earning a living,
he might feel less adequate as head of the family.

I hear the statement: "I'm afraid it would hurt my husband," or its equivalent—"I'm afraid it would hurt my husband's ego"—quite frequently as a form of resistance from women who contemplate a change in activity, and I always marvel at the *real* meaning of that message. For if a woman truly believes her growth and development will hurt her husband or damage his ego, this indicates her belief that his ego is so fragile it would be shattered by any external sign of growth. It implies that he's pretty weak and that she's potentially much stronger.

We don't hurt people by our growth. We *do* hurt them by our steadfast resistance to growth, because it makes us dried up and frequently resentful.

All my life I've wanted to travel. 'Course we couldn't. Well,
you know, my husband doesn't earn enough. That's all
right, though. I mean I don't mind. It's a man's
responsibility to earn a living for the family. But it's too late
now. I don't suppose I could enjoy it like I could have when
we were younger.

People who experience hurt feelings in relationship to *our* growth are persons who feel too inadequate to grow themselves. Our growth may remind them of their inability to risk change. But none of us gets a chance to grow if, by ignoring our feelings of discomfort, we forever protect those around us from theirs. If we choose to insist on our own right to grow, then we give everyone around us permission to do the same. We might even find that sharing what it means to risk growth and change, and to challenge fear and yet survive, opens up a whole new world of communication.

Guilt is our third big resistance to growth and change. And women seem to feel particularly guilty about almost everything.

21

Every time I go to an evening meeting, I feel guilty unless I get the kitchen cleaned up and the children in bed before I go. If I leave the place in a mess, I feel so bad I'm better off staying home.

≈

I feel guilty every time I say no to my husband when he wants sex. I just don't like to make love, but I feel like I'm under an obligation to do it anyway. I'd almost rather get the sex over with than feel guilty.

≈

I feel guilty every time I scream at the kids.

≈

I feel guilty whenever I go out and spend money. We don't have a lot, but why should I feel so damn guilty every time I go into a store?

≈

I feel guilty because I'm not happy most of the time. I know I should feel differently.

The list of guilts goes on and on. Women feel guilty if they do too much, or if they do too little. They feel guilty if they don't have sex often enough to suit their husbands' needs, or if they find themselves having sexual fantasies about other men. They feel guilty if they don't say "yes" to all the demands the various groups in our culture put on them, and guilty if they do say "yes" and neglect their jobs at home.

They're in a damned-if-you-do and damned-if-you-don't dilemma almost constantly. And if they seem to be less than perfect, they feel particularly guilty.

I've often asked groups of women to describe what they feel they *ought* to be in order not to feel guilty. The list usually looks like this:

I ought to be: A perfect wife, mother;

A gourmet cook when it comes to entertaining;

A perfect housekeeper, laundry lady;

A perfect accountant, prepared at all times with an accurate accounting of where the money went;

A perfect home repair expert and maintenance operator;

A perfect decorator on a penny-wise budget;

22

A perfect hostess, perfect in appearance (on a no-
money budget);
Perfectly able to handle crises of any kind;
Perfectly able to instill moral and religious values
in the children;
Perfectly in control of my own feelings;
Perfectly able to maintain the exterior of our prop-
erty, which means mowing the lawn, putting up
storm windows, etc.

But just pretty good in bed, not perfect because he might wonder
where I learned; or: It's not really nice to enjoy sex that much.
(When I've had the opportunity to question men's groups regarding the way men ought to be, the word perfect has never surfaced.)

Women tend to feel guilty because they don't do everything in
some kind of super fashion. And yet, when one analyzes the preparation most of us bring to marriage, it can scarcely be a surprise
we don't possess the extraordinary skills listed above.

I've puzzled over the problem of feminine guilt for a long time,
wondering about its origins. I'm beginning to be convinced that
most guilt is fear of punishment or fear of loss and relates to early
learned attitudes. All children learn quite early to feel guilty about
the pleasure they derive from touching their own bodies, which
becomes translated into feeling guilty about anything pleasurable.
Most children learn quite early that to work hard is to please mother
and father, and subsequently teachers and others in authority, so
they feel guilty if they're not engaged in something actively constructive. Most children learn to feel guilty about their hostile feelings toward parents, siblings, and friends, because these hostile
feelings could be potentially dangerous to them. And most girls per-
ceive very early that they should curb their aggressive feelings,
channeling them into more acceptable modes of behavior, which
means more ladylike behavior.

The message most girls receive, therefore, is that to be aggressive,
nonconstructive, and pleasure-seeking is not acceptable or OK . . .
so such behavior provokes guilt if it occurs. Conversely, to be nonaggressive, constructively active, and nonpleasure-seeking is rewarding and OK.

23

The fear of punishment aspect of guilt means, "I may be directly punished, or indirectly punished, by the loss of something or someone I care about."

As children, the loss of "someone that I care about" involved the loss of parental love. Children are highly vulnerable because of their dependency. To risk any behaviors that might cause our parents to become angry with us becomes dangerous or threatening to our safety. Or at least so we tell ourselves when we are children. Therefore, we try to curb our aggressive and pleasure-seeking impulses; we develop what Freud labeled a superego, that incorporated parental voice we call conscience, which helps us to control our impulses and delay our pleasures. Although Freud felt that women had relatively weakly developed superegos, my own experience with women is that they feel terribly guilty much of the time, about a wide variety of things. Feminine guilt seems particularly linked to feelings of independence and aggression.

As little girls, we learned to restrict particular behaviors in order to make certain our parents would continue to love and protect us, because we were sure we could not get along without their care. And there is a reality to that, for a period in our development. The problem for most women is that they continue to carry their dependency needs into adulthood and are quite convinced that they still need to be protected and cared about by others, who have now become substitute parental figures. Therefore, they must still restrict certain behaviors; they become acutely conscious of what others think of them, lest they find fault in them and reject them. Or they look to their children to give them the love they feel they need.

Whenever we restrict ourselves because we are afraid that we will lose someone's love, we are perpetuating the attitudes of the child within us who is afraid she couldn't get along in the world without someone to protect and care for her.

Whenever we operate from a posture of guilt and make impossible demands on ourselves, we create a situation in which life becomes a tedious overload, rather than something that we might enjoy.

Whenever we operate out of the fear that we won't be loved, we deny others the opportunity to know who we really are, and so *we don't get what we need at all.*

24

*If I'm not a good wife and mother, my kids will grow up and
not want to bother with me anymore.*

≈

*There are enough girls around the office where my husband
works who have nothing better to do than look gorgeous and
be totally interested in everything he says. So I can't afford
to not be perfect. He can always get whatever he wants
somewhere else.*

≈

*If I don't give in to my kid's demands, he'll hate me, or
he'll keep after me until I do give in.*

≈

*If I really let go—went back to school and let the housework
and all the other household crap just go for a while—
everyone would think I was a rotten wife and mother. I just
don't want people to think I don't care about my family.*

When we feel guilty it means we feel we don't have the right to
develop in whatever way is best for us. It says we *should* be something other than what we actually are. Many women run their
whole lives by *shoulds* and *oughts,* rather than by considering their
wants or *needs.*

Finally, women lay a lot of guilt on themselves because they take
the responsibility for everything that goes wrong in the family.

I know if anything goes wrong with the kids, it's my fault.

≈

*My husband's been offered a job in another city. I don't
want to move, but If I insist that we stay here, then it'll be
my fault if he doesn't advance in the company.*

≈

*I'm working now, but I still try to do everything at home just
like I did before I started working. If I didn't, I'd feel guilty.*

Guilty people are usually depressed people. Depressed people
are usually angry people. And angry people are usually frustrated
people. If you find yourself feeling a lot of guilt, take a look at
what's currently frustrating you or making you angry. Where do
you feel unsatisfied? What's not working right for *you?* And finally,
ask yourself what do you have to feel guilty about?

The one guilt I encourage women to feel is the one that concerns them directly. I think they *should* feel guilty if they're not dealing with themselves in a kind, direct way. I think they ought to feel guilty if they're taking out their frustrations and resentments on others, and not dealing directly with them themselves. I think they ought to feel guilty if they're merely existing, rather than living a life that has some rewards and promises for them. I think they ought to feel guilty if they neglect to follow their own dreams and desires, and instead place everyone else's needs and wants ahead of theirs.

Women need to find as many ways as possible to feel *good* about themselves, not *guilty*. For when a woman feels good about herself, everyone around her feels good too. When she feels guilty, everyone around her suffers from her constriction and pain. Guilty people have nothing to offer to anyone but their own guilt.

The final resistance we face in growing is perhaps the strongest. It raises the question: Do I really want to change? The problem with most of us is that it's a lot easier to remain in a kind of status quo situation; it's familiar, it's not fearful, and we know it quite well. Psychologists call this a repetition compulsion. We tend to repeat the same responses because they're familiar and we know them. It doesn't matter if they're constructive responses or not. It's as if we seek the familiar, regardless of how impossible, nonrewarding, or difficult the familiar is.

Raising the question, in itself, is a step toward growth. It means we acknowledge our tendency to want to repeat the familiar, and that we're aware we must challenge that tendency if we're to move toward growth and change.

I keep getting involved with guys who eventually drop me. It's happened so much I'm beginning to wonder if something isn't going on in me that makes me keep latching on to these guys who don't stay around for a more permanent relationship.

≈

I keep getting involved in real uproar scenes at home with my husband. It occurred to me that maybe I deliberately provoke these situations—even though I don't like them at all—because that's what went on at home all the time between my own parents.

≈

26

I tell everyone I want to go to work, but every time a job opportunity comes up I find some reason to turn it down. Maybe I don't want to work at all.

Whenever we *don't* go after what would make life easier, better, and more exciting, we must challenge the strength of this resistance, for what we're tacitly admitting is that we feel we don't deserve to have a happy, exciting, and rewarding life. We're perpetuating old familiar patterns of doing without; of playing it safe; of boxing ourselves in so we can't break free to savor what's certifiably good for us.

As children, we learned to be quiet, to be seen and not heard, to be docile, passive, and to defer to persons in authority. As adults, we can challenge these old ways of behaving. As adults, we have the right to be assertive, direct, and noisy, if necessary, in our quest for a better life for ourselves.

When we become assertively interested in pursuing a better life for ourselves, we're well on our way to becoming "grown up." For grown-ups do have the opportunity to get something for themselves, and having that experience means they have much more to give to those around them.

Resistances to growth are real. Whether it is fear, guilt, feelings of being selfish, or the fact that growth takes work and energy we'd rather not expend, we need to pay attention to our resistances; they are there to teach us lessons about life.

Take time to understand what your resistances are telling you. What are you really afraid of: That you might fail at something or that you might succeed? That you might lose someone's protection or that you might gain their respect?

What do you have to feel guilty about: That you didn't become what someone else wanted or that you didn't develop your own selfhood?

Resistances, like defenses, operate as a protection for us, to prevent us from feeling those things we are afraid to feel, or which we tell ourselves would be too dangerous to feel. But they prevent us from knowing ourselves and from letting others know us. They strongly limit our actions and restrict our choices.

When we begin to pay attention to them and to challenge their strength, it is because we are finally feeling strong enough to risk being honest with ourselves.

Then we can begin that special process which we call growth and change in order to become what we want to be, in fact what we *must* be, if we are to honor and respect the sum total that is us.

CHAPTER 4

Women and Their Parents

Throughout a lifetime, women have many special relationships. But there are some relationships that hold a much heavier weight than others in this process of growing up female. These are the relationships a woman holds with her parents, her children, and her husband. For it's out of these relationships that we discover the kind of persons we are and how we got that way.

We look in depth at the relationship we held with our parents, not in an accusatory way that places blame on them for not doing a good enough job with us, but rather to stand as observers and examine the way things were as we were growing up female.

No parent is perfect; and no child grows up without some holes in his or her development. Our job is to identify the holes so that we, as adults, can do something to fill them.

The major shaping of a woman probably occurs in her relationships with her parents or parent substitutes. Out of these relationships she learns she's a person of worth and value, capable of productive work and able to enter into loving relationships; or that she's relatively worthless, less than capable of work and quite incapable of holding loving relationships. It depends almost entirely on how her parents viewed themselves and their world.

If parents feel pretty good about themselves and are reasonably successful as human beings and family members, they're likely to transmit these good feelings to their children. If parents feel constricted, unhappy, trapped, or distressed, then *these* are the feelings they transmit to their children. Because parents represent the world to their children for a very long time, children are likely to grow up believing this is the way the world *is*.

It's almost as simple as this: If parents feel loved themselves, if they're getting a reasonable number of their own needs met, then they're likely to be able to deal in a loving fashion with their children. If their own needs have not been or are not being met, they'll have less to offer their children. It's the old pitcher model we talked about before: You can only pour out if there's something in the pitcher to pour. If the pitcher's dry, there's no way you can pour out anything.

You can test this out in your own experience. On days when you feel pretty good about yourself and your world, you usually have something good to offer others. On days when your world is out of focus, your giving is constrained, *if it's available at all*.

In a very simplistic model, I'm suggesting two things:

1. Most parents want to do a good job of parenting;
2. But parents can only do their job effectively if they're feeling relatively well satisfied with themselves.

When we're born we're utterly dependent on the good graces and wishes of our parents. Our needs as newborns are simple—we require food, care, love, clothing, and shelter. *But we cannot supply any of our own needs.* We're utterly dependent on our parents to supply those things for us. It sounds simple enough, but it isn't. For parents, well intentioned though they may be, frequently don't know exactly which need to try to satisfy, or are so hamstrung by their own unsatisfied needs they feel resentful about satisfying the needs of others.

An infant learns her own worth almost entirely by virtue of need satisfaction. If a child learns his parents usually will feed him when he's hungry, comfort him when he wants to be close, and tend to his physical and psychological well-being, the message to the child is clear: I'm cared for and cared about by these two special people in my life. I must be a person worth caring about, a person of value, since I can get people to care about me. And this feeling, originating in the parent-child relationship, can then be transferred to other persons who enter the child's life. If these others, by and large, care for and care about her, then this feeling of being of value is reinforced and continued, and probably will be sustained in most of her future relationships.

If, however, for whatever reasons, parents are unable to meet a child's needs, the message the child retains is equally clear: I'm *not* capable of being cared about and cared for; I *cannot* get people to satisfy my needs. And whenever a reinforcement of noncaring occurs in future relationships, it's absolutely confirmatory of what the child originally learned.

There are many reasons why parents can't meet a child's needs. There may be major economic difficulties placing a strain on the household. Father's job may require much moving or traveling. Father may not have a job. There may be health problems in the home; there may be psychological problems in the home. There may be problems with in-laws, neighbors, and friends. But a child doesn't know these things. All she knows is what occurs between herself and her parents. That's her whole world.

A child who's had good care and concern can tolerate some rejection as a normal function of the universe. A child who's been rejected in early crucial relationships will find each new instance of rejection intolerable. He may even, in future relationships, look for *any* signs of rejection to confirm what he believes to be true about himself: he's not worth caring about.

One of the difficulties we face as adults is that we tend to be repeaters of early experiences. They seem to have such a powerful impact on us; we almost seek them out, at least on an unconscious level, because they're so familiar.

It's essentially a matter of trust in these early months of life. If I've received what I needed from those significant persons on whom I depended, then I can move toward new relationships, anticipating that they'll also be trustworthy relationships. If I haven't experienced an initial, trusting parent-child relationship, then I'll tend to mistrust future relationships, *until proven otherwise*. And the proof may take a long time.

In my counseling relationships the issue of trust is the most important one faced, and not much progress can occur until trust is established. Trust is an almost infallible barometer of the quality of that original parent-child relationship. And the more it becomes a struggle for the individual and the therapist, the more it indicates how much mistrust and pain has been experienced by that person.

A woman I counseled with was the oldest of seven children. She'd received minimal caring, but more important, had to care for the other children as they came along, in a mother's helper role. When she married and had children of her own, she found herself increasingly angry and resentful. By the time her third child arrived, she'd run out of anything to give to anyone. Then she added guilt to her burden of feelings because she didn't feel happy about rejecting this child. Two children later she'd gained forty pounds and had become severely depressed.

Our job was to bring her first to an awareness that she could trust me with all her legitimate feelings of resentment, anger, and pain, and that her depression reflected a continued attempt to suppress these feelings.

When she could trust that I wouldn't reject her or make demands on her, then she could begin to face her own needs for love and caring that had so long been set aside in having to care for so many others.

The issue of trust returned in a second form. Could she trust that I truly cared about her? This is an even harder place to be, for it involves painful dependency feelings. As she could express her need for caring, and as she felt more dependent upon the caring that I could give her, would I someday withdraw my caring, causing her to be in more pain than ever? Could she trust my continued care?

When this level had been sustained, and she knew she could trust my continued caring, then, and only then, could she begin to look for outside sources in the world that could offer her some long overdue comfort. She could regard these outside relationships with less mistrust and consequently began to form significant friendships outside the therapy sessions.

Then she began to care about herself and for herself, which, in turn, reinforced the posture she presented to the outside world. And when she'd received enough caring from herself and others, then she really began to care about and for her children.

The problem of trust becomes complex when there's a death or divorce, or some kind of separation between parent and child. Frequently, children feel a mixture of anger, sadness, and guilt, which eventually attaches to future relationships, causing a continuous pattern of mistrust, based on the original painful separation.

I worked with a man whose mother died when he was three. He grew up receiving relatively good care from his father, but his relationships with women showed his continuing feelings about the death of his mother.

He'd remain somewhat aloof and distant, yet inwardly wanting to get closer and closer to the women he encountered, to somehow make up for his early loss.

When he finally conquered his distrust and fear, his need for closeness became overwhelming, and he frightened women away because of the intensity of his feelings. By the time he came to see me, he'd been severely hurt a number of times and was certain he'd never allow himself to become vulnerable to any woman again.

Our work became a constant testing of whether I would hurt him, as he felt every other woman had hurt him. When enough time had elapsed and the beginnings of trust were established, his original fear of the loss of something he loved came into awareness, and he became frightened that he'd lose me. Out of this emerged anger that he should be in such a vulnerable position, followed by painful feelings of guilt for having been angry with me.

Once he understood these were old feelings, placed on me, out of his original sense of loss, sadness for himself and anger about his loss finally emerged. As we shared this loss, and his subsequent need for mothering, we looked for other ways in which he could fulfill some of those needs for himself—ways of treating himself with care and concern that wouldn't place so much strain on a relationship with another woman.

With acceptance of his original loss and all attendant emotions, and with the understanding he'd never be able to replace that particular relationship, he began to form tentative relationships with much less intensity than before. Because he didn't have to be as aloof and distant, people responded more quickly to him, and he began to acquire more confidence in his ability to sustain a relationship.

The trust I'm talking about occurs most often in the relationship between a child and her mother. Trust is established at the beginning of life, and mother is usually the parent with whom an infant has most contact. Because the relationships between mother and child and father and child have different emphases, and since I believe there are some specific functions individual parents need to perform for their children, I think it's helpful to separate these parental roles. (See chapters 5 and 6.) Each parent has something specific to offer her or his child, and each of us is shaped by how well specific parental functions were performed.

After years of preparation a little girl emerges, ready to tackle the world and enter school. She's been through an intensive process of growth. She's not only experienced her own feelings, she's also literally taken her parental models into her own system, through a process called introjection, which means taking in, swallowing, ingesting parental attitudes, beliefs, and feelings as they're observed by her.

You might say that parenting is almost contagious for children. They catch it; they absorb it into their own internal systems, and they behave as if they have permanent mother figures and father figures dwelling within them. If you find this hard to believe, perhaps you've never seen a child relating to a friend, using exactly the same tone of voice, the same inflection, and the same gestures that are part of his or her parents' communication with the child or with others.

If parenting has been sick (of poor quality), then, quite literally, it can make a child sick. If parenting has been healthy, it can allow a child to be healthy.

Which brings us right back to what we said at the beginning of this chapter. Good parenting comes almost automatically from parents who feel good about themselves; who are fulfilling their own needs for affection, attention, recognition, and belonging and who can then satisfy the needs of others around them.

Good parenting also includes an understanding of the developmental phases kids go through, in order to facilitate, and not hinder, the growth process. Good parenting does *not* require expertise in child development. Good parenting does *not* require selfless sacrificing for the sake of the children.

Good parenting *does* require that we nurture and care for our children, set limits for their behavior, and that we find enough enjoyment and satisfaction in our lives to present a model of adulthood worth growing up for.

In addition, good parenting for a girl requires that her parents be sensitive to her need to be accepted as a female, of equal value and significance to the males around her. It also includes parental understanding of her need to be assertive in her femininity, and the appropriateness of her assertive behavior in gaining what she needs from life.

In particular, it places a demand on mother to do some good role modeling for her daughter of what it means to be an adult female. If mother's having a hard time gaining what she needs from life, the picture that's passed on and that her daughter introjects is that females, in fact, don't get what they want and need from life.

One woman I saw over a long period of time first came to me because she was unable to find any real satisfaction in life. She was dissatisfied with her husband, unhappy with her children, and was merely existing, without using any of the talents she possessed.

The picture of her mother that emerged was one of a totally unhappy female, unable to do anything, one who had little use for her children or husband, and who was scarcely able to pull herself together to maintain the home. Eventually, she couldn't even do that and settled into a deep depression, unable to care for herself.

Her daughter, my patient, at least had been able to remain functional. But each time she had the opportunity to engage in an activity that held meaning for her, she found herself filled with so much anxiety she could scarcely continue.

Our job was to challenge and ultimately evict that maternal model which had been introjected so long ago, and which persisted in interfering any time my patient wanted to be assertive and to express her own power.

In this case I could become a good therapist mother and could reinforce each occasion of assertive behavior until new patterns of action became automatic.

Parental introjects absorbed during early developmental years need to be examined, evaluated, and challenged if they don't fit with who we are. Those qualities of our parents that mesh with our self-concept and that are valuable to us ought to be kept and nurtured, with all the attendant good feelings that exist around them.

My mother was always interested in knowing what was going on in the world and insisted that we knew also. I'm really glad she did this, although when I was growing up I resented it at times, and there were other things I wanted to do.

≈

My father was firm with us, but underneath that gruffness we knew he really cared. I'd like to be the same kind of parent.

≈

My parents' strictness—which I hated in high school—was probably the one thing that kept me out of trouble. I'd never let my kids run around without any discipline, like some parents do.

Those parental introjects that we don't want to use as models for ourselves can be discarded—*if we work at it.*

My mother worked all the time. There was never any time for the children: just her job, then the household chores. I find myself automatically going about life in the same work-oriented fashion, and I'm trying to break that pattern. It's hard and I don't do a very good job of it, but at least I'm trying.

≈

My dad believed in hitting a kid first and asking questions second. I was shocked when I realized I was doing the same thing with my own kids, even though I knew how painful it had been for me. I've got to find a better way to deal with my kids, because I can't stand living with the guilt I feel.

The entire reason for examining our relationships with our parents in detail is that we may, in fact, focus on what *we choose to be like* as adults. If we never examined what we bring with us, we'd never have a chance to learn what it is we need and how to choose ways to fill those needs.

We'd continue in repetitive patterns, doing what we don't choose to, not getting what we really want, forever driven by our introjected parents, who still view us as children needing guidance.

36

Growing up means choosing *our own* way—the way unique to us. It also means saying good-bye to the parent within, so a new history might be written. We may feel empty inside at first, because we've grown accustomed to those parental introjects; or because we've grown used to projecting those old parental feelings onto current people we make into new parents for us.

But if we are to say good-bye successfully to the parent who resides within us, we must also recognize and separate from the *child* within, who insists that the world continue to parent us as we have become accustomed to being parented. When we examine our relationships with our parents, we are able to separate what they actually *were* for us from what we wanted them to *be* for us.

Then we can accept the reality of the past and the present that *we* now might direct the future.

CHAPTER 5
Women and Their Mothers

Trust between infant and mother is established in the mutuality of their relationship. It's almost as if they need to establish a language of communication unique to them. Ask any mother of a newborn and she'll tell you there's a difference between the cry of a child who's hungry, one who's fussy, or one who's uncomfortable. But mother must learn that language, and the difficulty for her is that she has to learn it on her own. Each child has a different way of communicating, and every new mother and child must reach an understanding of how to communicate with each other.

So one of the first lessons a newborn learns is to make demands on this world by active, assertive yelling, in order to feel better. If it works and she gets an appropriate response to her particular need, then the beginnings of trust have been established, and eventually she'll acquire the capacity to wait for relief . . . at least a little. If she doesn't get a response to her needs, she'll find waiting almost unbearable.

There was a time when we put infants on rigorous feeding schedules, never deviating from the time of feeding, no matter how hungry a child might become. I'm convinced this forced waiting produced a whole generation of adults who get uneasy and anxious whenever they're dependent on someone else to fill a need, for fear it won't really happen. Most people find it hard to be in a dependent position (which is really the stance of the helpless newborn).

One of my patients was afraid of hospitals—motivated to do almost anything to stay away from them. Once inside them, she became engulfed in anxiety for fear she wouldn't be able to get away.

Her mother had been ill when she was born, and she'd been cared for by a series of mother substitutes, with her actual mother not regaining good health for several years. Her father traveled a great deal, and she had no brothers or sisters.

The hospital, which represented the home she came from, created enormous fear in her that she wouldn't receive care, as had been her experience. Trust for her was nonexistent when it came to depending on someone else to take care of her.

These early feelings of dependency are a natural part of infancy and early childhood experiences for all of us. They become difficult for us, as adults, when our early needs were somehow ignored or when we couldn't trust that we would be taken care of. The problem for us now is that dependency needs come out of a very early time in our lives when we were operating at a preverbal level with the world around us. Therefore, we couldn't tell people what we wanted; we couldn't ask for what we needed; we couldn't describe our discomforts except by crying. Even then there was no guarantee that someone would respond properly.

Consequently, these early experiences and their attendant feelings get stored away, unlabeled except by their discomfort, and emerge at later times, when we least expect them.

I don't know what was wrong, I just found myself feeling very uncomfortable.

≈

I have no reason not to trust her; but there's something that seems not quite right when I'm with her.

≈

All of a sudden I became very anxious. My heart started pounding; I was afraid I would faint. I don't know what happened. I just got very frightened—over nothing.

≈

40

*I know it's crazy, but I'm afraid to go out of the house. I'm
fine inside, but every time I have to go anywhere I go crazy. I
just can't do it. It's like I'm afraid of everything in the
outside world.*

Trust and dependency go hand in hand. Unknown, unexpected,
unlabeled fear and anxiety frequently come out of this very early
time in our lives when we had to trust our caring to other persons.
Upon that early dependency rests our initial impressions of the
world outside of us, as to its reliability and caring or its capricious-
ness and noncaring. How much trust we feel in ourselves and in
others around us has roots in our earliest years of life, at a time
when we were most vulnerable.

This is not to even suggest a mother has to respond instantly and
perfectly to every cry of her child. It's rather to state that mother
and baby must establish a kind of ritual between them that says:
"We understand each other." Once this ritual is established, a
child has a distinct chance to learn to trust the world around her: If
I can establish it with mother, then I can establish it with others.
Mother represents, and really *is*, the world for this newborn. She's
the nurturer and comforter, and by her caring she gives an explicit
message that this child is worth caring about. Father may also function in these roles, and there's no question that it would be exceedingly helpful to everyone if he were able to share in a more active
way. It would take the exclusive burden off of mother and would
add immeasurably to a child's sense of well-being to get a second
dose of nurturing and caring. But because of father's frequent ab-
sence from home, he's not as available as mother to meet the infant's needs. If we, as a society, took seriously the fact that early
fathering is necessary to the health of the child, perhaps we'd set
up conditions for father to be home more often.

As it stands now, the burden of these crucial early messages of
self-worth hangs on mother's tired shoulders. It's a difficult burden, and I frequently talk to mothers who feel overloaded by this
responsibility.

*If anything goes wrong, it's my fault. My husband's only
around on weekends. I've got all the responsibility, and it's
really bugging me.*

≈

41

I feel so afraid I'll ruin my child's life forever. I can't stand living with the guilt that I may be wrecking my child.

Mother can provide only as much trust and love as she's taking in for herself. If her supply is short, she'll have very little to give. Some women are uncomfortable as mothers, right from the start.

One woman with whom I worked had her first child almost precisely nine months after she was married. She found herself not only resenting the pregnancy, but feeling awkward and hateful toward her child once he arrived.

In her own family she was the oldest of four children, three of whom were born in fewer than three years. She'd had scarcely any contact with her mother, who was a semidepressed alcoholic. As mother had more children and became more depressed, this child became increasingly responsible for the family. Her relationship with mother became a complete role reversal. By the time she came to see me, her child was five years old, and she was still resentful about his presence, as well as feeling awkward as a mother. Although she'd had a great deal of experience in taking care of children, she'd never learned to trust that initial relationship with her mother, and she still carried forward the pain and frustration of that first relationship and her continued need to experience solid mothering herself before she could become a successful mother.

In our relationship the issue of trust was long in developing. Only when she could finally trust me could she begin to drop her guardedness in relation to her child. Then she began to be more spontaneously affectionate with him, which pleased and delighted them both. Children have a marvelous way of responding to warmth, whenever it occurs. Almost any gesture of fun or friendship will be responded to if children feel it's real.

And interestingly enough, as she learned to experience trust, her appearance changed considerably. She became quite lovely *as she emerged as a* loving *person.*

In addition to their nurturing role, I think mothers have three major functions in the lives of their children.

1. As primary love object; that is, the first person the child experiences in a loving relationship;
2. As a source of identification for future feminine behavior for daughters, and as a model of what females are all about for sons;
3. As the adult female in the family who offers *acceptance* to the *growing* female in the family, in the latter's attempts to mature and become an adult.

Mother is the first person children encounter in their beginning attempts at relationships. As such, she offers a baseline in expectations. She's the one who provides pleasure; the one who offers direct skin-to-skin touching contact; the one who strokes; the one who lets her child know, by actual contact, that it's good to feel good; it's good to feel close; it's good to feel pleasure; it's good to love. This is the beginning of intimacy, and it has a crucial relationship to our capacity to experience intimacy as adults.

If mother feels *reasonably* nurturant, caring, and loving, if she's comfortable being close, the infant can directly experience a loving relationship. But if she feels constrained, angry, anxious, or resentful, should her own caring needs be unfulfilled for whatever reason, then she's distinctly limited in her capacity to offer anyone else a loving relationship.

Children sense this. They intuitively know how much mother has to offer them. Yet, they seem to become even more demanding and anxious if they don't receive what they need, which may make mother even more angry and resentful, and create further discontent and guilt for everyone.

Children have a variety of ways of making demands on us, just when we are least capable of meeting such demands.

Why is it every time I get on the telephone my child starts to ask me questions or to make requests—anything to get my attention?

≈

Each time we're ready to go out, the uproar begins. It's like they've got an unerring sense of our leaving and store up trouble, waiting for the one moment when all I want is to get out.

≈

*What is there about bedtime? I go through a ritual every
night, but it's always something more that they want:
another story, another drink, another hug. At that point I've
had it! I don't have anything more to give.*

A primary love relationship, as well as any loving relationship,
demands a mutuality among partners, a giving and receiving that
enhances and enriches the relationship. Child cries; mother re-
sponds; child feels better; mother feels better as a mother; both feel
satisfied, which is to say, both feel good. That's what loving is all
about.

If mother is able to satisfy these early needs in her role as a primary love object, it's only because she's reasonably well satisfied
with herself. Being well satisfied with self means paying attention to
her own needs as well as to the needs of her child. Some women
get caught in a masochistic place when they become mothers. They
seem to feel that they have to devote all their time and energies to
the care and maintenance of this newborn, sacrificing themselves
until they are exhausted. It's the old problem of feminine guilt
again. What will people think of me as a mother? Will I ruin my
child if I don't . . . ?

When we have children and are called upon to care for this dependent new life, our own needs for caring are revived and in-
creased. Therefore, it becomes crucial that we experience sufficient
supportive relationships, *for us,* that we might expend the amount
of caring called for in the early months of life, for another.

Women who do not recognize and pay attention to their own
needs pay a high price in the quality and quantity of their caring. A
cared-for mother can do a lot of caring. Discontented, uncared-for
mothers produce discontented children.

Mother also serves as a source of feminine identification for her
daughter. A girl will model her behavior after her mother's behavior, particularly if she judges mother's behavior to be relatively successful. If Mom looks reasonably happy and excited about life, then
she appears to be a pretty good model to follow. Children enjoy
being like successful parents. It makes them feel they have a chance
at being the same way. Unfortunately, children also model after us
in our least successful moments, and this kind of modeling is as
unsuccessful for them as it is unsuccessful behavior for us.

Our parents modeled for us, that is, they were our first and most important models of what it meant to be a woman or a man. If mother believed being a woman was something worthwhile, chances are we'll feel somewhat the same way. But if mother was convinced being a woman was not worthwhile, or that men have all the advantages, then she's likely to transmit that same message to a daughter, who can, in turn, carry on a similar disadvantaged position in her future relationships.

Modeling femininity is really modeling an attitude, rather than a specific kind of behavior. What it means is that if Mom is comfortable as a woman, it doesn't matter what specific behavior she follows. Her daughter is likely to see that being female is an exciting possibility for her too. Mom can be turned on by homemaking or be content to remain, generally, around the home; or she can be turned on by a career and devote only a specific amount of time to being around the house; or she can be whatever it is that turns her on. It's the quality of being turned on *toward* something in life that makes a woman a successful model of femininity for her daughter. Being turned on means being excited, interested, and involved in something that gives her a sense of well-being and fulfillment. It's a quality, an essence, rather than a specific kind of behavior. If it's *real*, then it's contagious, and essential in a daughter's need both to identify with her mother and to value what it means to be female.

Perhaps the most crucial step in development for a girl rests in being *accepted* by her mother. A daughter goes through a difficult growing-up period, somewhere between the ages of three and six, in which she turns from mother toward father, essentially changing her affections in an open and direct way. In psychological language this change in love object is called the Oedipal conflict. It indicates a normal shifting of affection from the parent of the same sex (Mom) to the parent of the opposite sex (Dad), in order to form a girl's first heterosexual love relationship. It's particularly painful for mother and daughter because their relationship can become strained as it's set aside in favor of this newer and more exciting relationship with father.

The situation is resolved easily in homes where mother and father care about each other. After a fairly intense time of daughter "courting" father, daughter gives up on Dad and turns back to Mom to continue her normal development as a female and to resume normal mother/daughter contacts. Simply stated, the child recognizes that mother and father have a pretty good thing going and her best chance is to grow up and find her own husband (daddy) for herself.

It becomes essential that mother understand her daughter's striving for father's attention as well as her daughter's subsequent need for acceptance and recognition from mother as a resolution for this critical time in development.

Resolution of the Oedipal conflict has two distinct phases for a daughter.

1. Giving up her claim on father and recognizing the stability of mother's and father's relationship;
2. Receiving acceptance from mother that she is still loved and respected by mother and is affirmed as a growing-up female by the female who has already done it.

But it's difficult for most women to realize that this is a temporary state of affairs, absolutely necessary for growth to occur. And most mothers find it difficult to experience the rejection they feel coming from their own daughters. There's almost a sense of disbelief.

After all I've done for her [quite literally true], how could she talk about hating me?

And there's frequently anger and resentment.

I sure don't deserve all the crap she dishes out. It's almost like my daughter and I are in competition for my husband. Sometimes I feel like she's winning.

And of course, it *is* a real form of competition that emerges at this time between mother and daughter. By virtue of her growth process, a daughter is literally propelled away from Mom and toward this relationship with her father. What she may not be prepared for is her mother's response to this competition. If Mom has had difficulty with competition herself, if she feels like she generally loses when competing, then she isn't going to like being in competition with her *own* daughter in her *own* home over her *own* husband. If Mom has never resolved the problem of her *own* Oedipal conflict

46

(if she's still trying to resolve it by giving up on Dad and regaining her own mother's acceptance), then her daughter's behavior will likely produce a flood of old, painful feelings to make the situation even more complicated.

Some mothers never grant this crucial acceptance to their daughters. They never get past the competition, and they simply refuse to acknowledge their daughters as grown up.

One of the women with whom I worked was in her late forties and was still trying to gain her mother's acceptance. Mother still treated her in all ways as a little girl, incapable of handling her own family, and she constantly interfered with my patient's life, insisting, in a very "kind" way, that she didn't know how to do "it" right. My patient was nearly torn apart by wanting to be allowed to be an adult woman and still remain loyal to her mother, treating her with some respect. She experienced enormous guilt for the rage and resentment she felt toward this woman who wouldn't allow her to grow up.

As the story emerged, mother and father had had an extremely impoverished marriage, with father going outside of the marriage, on several occasions, to other women.

It began to appear that mother, who was experiencing so much competition from other women, couldn't allow this daughter to win in any competition with her because of the pain she felt regarding these adult rivals winning father's affection. By keeping her daughter little and incapable, at least she won one competition.

During this Oedipal time a daughter will continue to solicit the loving affection of father until she learns she isn't going to be able to replace mother, after all, in father's affection. Eventually, she gives up her claim on father and resolves that if she learns to be like mother, perhaps *one* day she'll have a husband all her own, with no competition from anyone (until she has her own daughter!).

With this, a daughter turns back toward mother for additional caring and further identification. But having rejected Mom for a while, there's considerable fear Mom won't be available as a loving, good parent anymore, and that Mom won't accept her back after all the difficulty between them. *And then she'll have nobody.*

It's a scary time, and one in which mothers and daughters can come very close together if they can overcome the competition and separateness the Oedipal period foisted upon them.

If mother has some strength and confidence in herself as a woman, she'll have a much higher tolerance for competition from her daughter, and she can also view this rivalry with some degree of pride as a sign of growth and development. If Mom has something going for herself, she won't be torn apart by her daughter's rejection. *And* she'll be able to offer the acceptance her daughter so badly needs to prove she's understood and cared about, in spite of her changing affections.

But if Mom is unable to feel some competency as a woman, she'll scarcely be able to tolerate her daughter's competition, let alone forgive her, and she'll never allow her to grow up.

Without acceptance from mother, a daughter is forced to seek any kind of acceptance she can find, as a female. There remains, however, a loneliness and an isolation exceedingly difficult to overcome. The kind of acceptance she may gain from a peer group will never quite substitute for the basic acceptance a mother can offer a daughter that says quite simply: "I'm glad that you're growing up as a woman; I'm proud of your growth, and I anticipate that you'll grow into a loving and competent woman in your own right and *in your own way.*"

That kind of acceptance is the most important stability we can offer our daughters. Without it, they may search endlessly for a "good mother," perhaps never finding one. With it, they're well on their way toward growing up . . . *female.*

What was your mother like? Did she enjoy being a woman? Did she enjoy being a wife? How did she prepare you for being a woman? Did you ever feel she accepted you as an adult woman, capable of functioning as an equal?

In many ways this mother-daughter relationship is the most crucial, as well as the most difficult, relationship we face. The combination of intense love, competition, rejection, and the need for acceptance are powerful emotions to cope with at any age.

If we are to feel competent as women, we need to look very carefully at the first woman in our life from whom we learned so many lessons.

I never wanted to be like my mother. She was cold and complaining, and I hated her most of the time. It was frightening to me the first time I found myself talking and acting just like her with my own children. I couldn't believe it!

≈

My mother was always quiet, hardly said a word. She didn't have many friends, and she seemed uncomfortable most of the time. I was always just the opposite—outgoing, lots of good friends until I got married and had children. All of a sudden I found myself withdrawing more and more. I became frightened and anxious, something I had never experienced before. I didn't know who to turn to or what to do.

≈

I could never please my mother. I just never did anything good enough to get any kind of recognition from her that I was OK. She's been dead for a long time but not forgotten. There's nothing I do now for myself that pleases me. Oh, it's OK, but it's nothing special. It's as if she's still around and I'm still not good enough, but this time it's me that's not satisfied.

These early imprints of behavior are built into our being, although many of them are on an unconscious level. They emerge and surprise us with their unexpectedness and their intensity. We find ourselves behaving very much like our mothers and doing those things we liked *least* in them.

Only when we examine this relationship will we be able to separate ourselves from our mothers. Then we will be free to be ourselves. We can value and retain those characteristics of mother that we felt good about and which seem to fit us. We can reject those parts that are foreign to us because they do not belong to us.

As a psychologist who is a woman, I am often set in a mothering place by those who come to see me. There is no question that our initial relationship is a barometer of that first relationship. When mother has been reasonably warm and open, the possibilities for trust are almost immediate. When mother has seemed guarded, distant, hostile, or unavailable, trust in our relationship develops very slowly and is tested many times.

Most of the women I work with would like to have had more mothering that was an accepting kind of experience. Most of them doubt their competency as adult women, which means they don't feel quite grown up yet. Many of them feel they remained unaccepted and unrecognized by their mothers once that early separation had occurred in their childhood. Without sensing their mothers' understanding and respect for their growth and development, it was very difficult to give themselves permission to feel good about who they were and what they were becoming.

Perhaps one of the most important reasons women need to come together in groups is to gain acceptance and concern *from one another,* which is an up-to-date version of mothering.

CHAPTER 6

Women and Their Fathers

A girl has a different relationship with her father. In many ways it's prototypical of future relationships with other men. And in many other ways it's special. It doesn't have the elements of competition and rejection that are present in the mother-daughter relationship. It doesn't include the intense dependency that existed in the early mother-infant relationship. Rather, father stands as the parent who leaves home and makes an impact on the outside world, then comes home as protector of the household.

He's the provider, but he provides by assertively acting in the world, by having a job. Although many women work today and actively support the household, most *young* children still experience mother as being more at home with the children, and father as actively working outside the home.

Father has a kind of mystique about him that involves having a place to go and spending time away from the family. Some children don't even know where their fathers go during the day, but daddy goes, and a great deal of time in a young child's life is spent waiting for him to come back.

For the young child, father is a kind of mystery. He's gone long enough during the day for the child to build up a kind of expectation of what's going to happen when he returns. But he comes home in varying ways: sometimes happy, sometimes tired; sometimes angry, sometimes depressed; sometimes on time, sometimes

51

late. Sometimes he's friendly, sometimes he says, "Go away, I'm too tired." We've moved away from the stance of father as punisher when he gets home. But most young children interact only occasionally with their fathers, compared to the time spent with their mothers.

Consequently, what father brings back into the house with him speaks very loudly to a growing child about what the world outside the home is like. Father's capacity to have made a satisfactory life for himself in the world, his ability to make demands and make an impact on the world outside, is a powerful influence on the meaning of adulthood for a child.

Because our growth patterns always move us toward that time when we will leave home also, father's capacity to do just that becomes crucial to us as potential adults. If father's reasonably satisfied with his situation in the working world, chances are we'll also expect to feel reasonably satisfied when we leave home. If father's a failure or isn't available, there remains a great area of doubt as to our capacity to make an impact on that world outside, which means getting what we want and need as adults, in an assertive and direct way.

What I'm saying is that there are two kinds of roles that must be modeled for children, that they might incorporate them *both* into their life-styles: one kind of nurturing role which represents comfort and caring, and another kind of assertive role which represents growth and independence. These are the two polarities out of which we operate most of our lives: the need to be close and the need to be separate; the need to be dependent and the need to be independent. *Both roles can be modeled by both parents.* Both kinds of behavior are necessary in developing our ability to act as competent and complete adults.

If a woman has received inadequate fathering due to loss of father (death or divorce) or due to father's inability to offer this kind of role model, her ability to handle herself as an adult woman may be severely interfered with in various ways having to do with asserting herself in the world.

One of my patients had a great deal of difficulty in saying no to anyone or anything. Her father died when she was five.

52

*Mother never remarried, so she never had a relationship with
a male that would substitute for a father.*

*Consequently, she always found herself acting in a
nurturing role with the rest of the world, and* her nurturing
didn't include being able to say no.

Our dialogues frequently went like this:

> Patient: I got a call today asking if I'd serve on the PTA
> board. And you know, I went through the same
> lousy freeze I always do. I started to feel tight
> inside and panicky. I don't want to do it, but I get
> caught in that awful place that says someone
> ought to do it, and that I could probably squeeze
> it in.

> Therapist: What did you tell yourself would happen if you
> said no?

> Patient: That they wouldn't like me if I didn't do it. It's
> the same old garbage. I say yes because I'm
> afraid to say no.

> Therapist: And then you get angry with yourself?

> Patient: Absolutely . . . but if I don't say yes, I feel guilty.
> It's being nowhere. I can't win either way.

*Our job will be to work on building self-confidence so she
can risk being assertive and independent, which means
getting what she wants, without feeling she'll be rejected for
her behavior.*

In addition to modeling assertive behavior, father also has a specific function to perform in terms of the development of femininity
in a little girl. Watch a three-year-old girl with almost any adult
male who's friendly, and you'll see the beginnings of femininity in
action. She'll flirt, laugh, and try to get as close as possible to that
big friendly male. It's her nature to respond in a different way to
Dad than to Mom because he serves as her first love object of the
opposite sex. If he's able to respond with kindness and warmth to
these first female attempts to attract a male, she'll begin to develop
feelings of confidence and a sense of her potential power in future
relationships with males.

However, if father's uncomfortable with these sudden assertions
of aggressive warmth and affection (which frequently include wanting to marry him by first getting rid of mother!), and if he doesn't

know how to respond, this petite female will begin to doubt her capacity to attract a male, thereby limiting her future ability to look over a wide variety of males before making long-term commitments. Or perhaps she'll look toward other ways to get father's attention. One of these, unfortunately, might include denying her femininity, believing father would prefer her to be something other than what she is.

One of my patients, an only child, had a father who was quiet, and ill at ease with his feelings. He wasn't antagonistic to his daughter but was unable to get close to her, and he was quite defensive whenever she came near. With her growing needs for closeness unsatisfied, she learned, as a young child, to do those things that he enjoyed doing, that were predominantly male-oriented. She'd go fishing with him, go to sporting activities with him, and, in general, modeled her behavior after his.

She thus became, in many ways, the son he didn't have. This worked pretty well until she became an adolescent and found she wasn't like other adolescent girls. She'd "attracted" her father by denying she was a girl, but that kind of tactic was highly self-defeating to the adolescent, sexual feelings that began to emerge in her.

Being a "boy" didn't help her get dates. Denying her femininity kept her from feeling comfortable with girls her own age. She retreated to the safety of father's company but began to feel more anxious and isolated than ever. She started gaining weight and soon became too frightened to leave the house.

Father, in desperation, contacted me. When I first saw her she was quite boyish in appearance, dressed in jeans with short, cropped hair, and most unattractive. She was ill at ease, much as father was ill at ease with women. Our job was to retrace the steps toward her original decision to be a "boy" for her dad, in order to gain his approval and love, and then to move toward an acceptance of her own feminine nature, denied for such a long time.

Because of her need to be close to him, she was willing to sacrifice anything—even her own self, but the sacrifice had totally stunted her growth.

54

One can see similar kinds of behavior in homes where there are sons around. If father is more comfortable with the males in the household, a girl could get a powerful message that it's much better to be like her brothers. She may find herself resenting the fact she was born a girl; or she may feel angry and resentful toward any and all males for not giving her what she really wanted, which was an acceptance and regard for who she was, without having to change anything.

Being feminine and being assertive are highly linked to each other, and both are deeply interwoven in a girl's relationship with her father. In the past we usually associated femininity with nonassertive, or even passive behavior. Typically, masculine was aggressive, active, and independent; feminine was nonaggressive, passive, and dependent. Girls learned very early to curb their aggressive natures, in order to fit into what they viewed as appropriate, cultural, feminine behavior.

But when we look at developmental models of children, we find that girls exhibit at least as much, if not more, aggressive and assertive behavior than boys during preschool years. It's only when girls are acculturated through the school system that they begin to express their aggression less directly.

All children begin to be assertive sometime during their second year of life, as a part of normal human development. After they've learned to trust their environment, they have to test their strength against it in order to feel their autonomy.

Shortly after this thrust toward independence begins, little girls start to experience and express their femininity, particularly regarding their fathers. And so, developmentally, assertiveness and sexual expression occur almost contemporaneously. If father can understand and be comfortable with his daughter's emerging sexuality, as well as her attempts at assertive, autonomous behavior, without being threatened by them, these two important phases of growth can occur and develop in a relatively normal fashion. It's normal and natural for a little girl to express loving feelings toward her father that are assertive and sexual. But if father's frightened by his daughter's assertive sexuality, if he ignores her need for acceptance as a female, she may learn to fear and mistrust her own femininity, or become even more assertive in her demands for greater attention

55

from him. If father's not available, she may spend her whole life searching for an accepting father in *every* future relationship with males.

> *One of my patients was a competent, intelligent, attractive woman, in her early thirties, who appeared to be quite successful. There were times, however, when she felt quite disabled and in need of protection. When she was three her father left her mother, and she had had no contact whatever with him since that time. She grew up and appeared to be well adjusted, but part of her still operated at age three, particularly in relation to men. She would lose her confidence and ability to act as a responsible adult woman, and would have strong desires to get close and be warm and safe. Because she was an adult woman, such warmth and closeness inevitably produced strong sexual feelings. When that occurred she was overwhelmed with a flood of emotions, causing her to cry most painfully. Part of her desperately wanted the warmth of a daddy; part of her responded as an adult woman. The result was a painful conflict in which neither state could be satisfied.*
>
> *Our work was to acknowledge and accept the existence of this three-year-old part of her that wanted and needed warmth and protection and that felt angry and frightened because of her loss. Our job was also to separate past from present, to help her to find satisfactions in her adult sexual relationships, as well as to find ways to comfort and protect the child within her who felt so hurt and abandoned.*

But if father actually gets involved in his daughter's emerging sexuality and acts seductively in return, she may lose any incentive to grow at all.

> *One woman I worked with, who was in her early twenties, was the beloved daughter of a man who'd been behaving in a very seductive way with her since early childhood. She didn't get along with her mother, who was a cold, rejecting woman. Consequently, both she and her father turned to each other for warmth and affection. By the time she entered adolescence there was no question where father's affection centered. If there'd ever been any competition with mother over father, mother had lost long ago.*

*Although the relationship was never consummated
sexually, it was obviously a very intimate one. She went all
through high school and college without dating at all,
remaining very attached to Dad.*

*When she was twenty-three she seemed to enter
adolescense a second time. She became heavier, her face
broke out, she had crying spells; she behaved in a typically
adolescent way and had emotional ups and downs.*

*Concurrently, she made no attempts to get a job, move
away from home, or establish any other kind of relationship.*

*Mother finally insisted something be done to help her
grow up. I'm convinced her second adolescence occurred
as a kind of second chance to grow and separate from Dad—
something she'd been unable to do before.*

A girl in her Oedipal period turns toward father as her love object
as a natural and normal part of the growth process. But she needs
to learn that father, in fact, will not change in his loyalty to mother,
and that *her* only hope lies in someday finding a husband of her
own to be close to, as mother and father are close to each other.

However, if a daughter should win in her competition with
mother, which means she gets father away from mother, she is presented with major problems that may be long-lasting and difficult to
solve. She's likely to have strong guilt feelings about mother; she
might fear mother could retaliate for this loss and make life difficult
for her. If she's already won the battle for father, she'll also have
no reason to turn toward other heterosexual relationships to satisfy
her growth needs. She's likely to remain stuck somewhere around
a five-year-old level, fearful of mother's disapproval but unable to
be freed from father.

*A woman came to see me with the complaint that she always
felt like a child in her relationships with other adults. Even
though she was in her early forties she found herself forever
trying to please the adults around her, but never feeling like
an adult herself. She'd grown up in a family where mother
was sick and unavailable most of the time. She and father
transferred their affections to each other.*

*Although she was married, she was unable to feel very
involved sexually with her husband. She still longed for the*

protection and devotion father had showed her. She wanted very much for her husband to assume this fatherly role.

When she had children she became resentful of their demands. She experienced both fear and anger toward her mother, which she felt she couldn't express, plus a continuing need to hang on to father.

Her husband, sensing her preference for father, was rapidly becoming disenchanted with the marriage. Because of her sexual rejection he became even more distant, sending her back to father, who was still more than willing to supply comfort and love.

Until she could give up her claim on father, and the belief that he could give her more than her husband, there was little hope the marriage could survive.

There are three stances for a father to take toward his growing daughter that I think are crucial.

1. An understanding of and affection for the normal development of her assertiveness and femininity;
2. Assistance in providing limits and structures for these emerging feelings, so they can become understood and controlled; that is, so that they don't become overwhelming;
3. Assurance for his daughter that she stands in a parent-child relationship to him, *not* in a husband-wife relationship, and that he can be relied upon to consistently behave in this fashion toward her.

A father who is able to deal openly and affectionately with his daughter provides a crucial model for psychosexual development. If a daughter has had a reliable and loving relationship with an adult male, she is able to develop a trust and confidence in her ability to form other successful relationships with males. Without such trust she is likely to insist on serious one-to-one relationships when she begins dating, fearful of any competition. Later, when she becomes interested in marriage, she will probably choose the first male that asks her, rather than postpone her choice until she has had a chance to develop fully her own sense of self.

Women who have not had adequate fathering often feel a sense of inadequacy as women, which they believe will only be resolved by attaching themselves to men who make them feel better, or through whose achievements they can vicariously gain some good feelings for themselves.

Father also stands as an authority figure and serves as a model for future attitudes toward other such persons. If father is critical and punishing, a daughter may see other authority figures as likely to hurt her and will feel automatically defensive in their presence.

If father has a sense of his own well-being, if he has been in touch with his own struggle for growth and development, he will be able to accept his daughter's need to grow. And he will be able to provide those structures and limits that allow her to grow.

All children need some sense of structure around them to act as a protection against unlimited freedom and choice. It is as if we need something to test our muscles against to make sure those muscles actually exist.

If father is uncertain about himself, or if he has never tested the limits of his own parents, then he will have more difficulty in providing the kinds of structures that are needed. At first, as parents, we protect our children, lest they harm themselves physically. Later, we help them to incorporate a sense of freedom *and* control, lest they are harmed emotionally.

Good fathering allows a daughter to express her assertiveness and femininity on schedule and to find these to be acceptable and normal feelings. It provides her with the protection of someone who cares enough to set limits on the free expression of such feelings, as an affirmation that society *does* set limits on expressions of feelings. And by *not* winning in her competition with mother, it allows a daughter to give up her claim on father, form a feminine identification with mother, and ultimately transfer her affection to a boy of her own choice.

What was your father like? How close were you able to be with him? What did you do together? How did he treat your mother? If you had brothers, did he have a preference?

Most of the women in my groups would have liked more *closeness* with their fathers. They felt a distance and an awkwardness that they regretted. They'd have liked more time together and less distance between them. But they weren't convinced that their mothers and fathers were very close, which somehow was akin to their relationship with their fathers, and they felt as though they'd missed something.

59

CHAPTER 7

Women and Their Children

Just about the time we're supposed to be grown up, we usually start having children of our own. And we're confronted with the amazing fact that the advent of our own children revives some old childhood conflicts, bringing them back to the surface of consciousness, from where they'd long since been buried. Instead of acting as "mature" adult parents, we find ourselves engaging in power struggles with our two-year-old and in verbal or physical battles with our four-year-old; we behave childishly while we try to deal as parents with our children. It's almost as if our old conflicts emerge in living color in our own homes, regardless of what we do to stop them.

As our children grow they remind us, at each stage of *their* development, of what we were like in *our* development. We may not remember precise events from our past, but we'll recognize something of what it was like by the intensity of our current feelings.

The incredible part of all this is that this rerun of our childhood enables us to have a second chance to grow up properly. We can learn about our own growing up while our children are growing up, if we're willing to give ourselves the opportunity.

We might discover that some of the things which bug us about our children are the things we, as children, would love to have done but weren't allowed to.

I'd been brought up in a very rigid, punitive household in which no one ever defied an authority of any kind. When my two-year-old daughter decided to assert herself and defiantly said, "I won't!" it really made me mad. Who was she to be talking to me like that? I was furious, and the more I fumed, the more stubborn she got. I'd never have gotten away with that.

≈

I have a hard time with my daughter's sexual behavior. She's only three, but she's curious about everything having to do with sex. She obviously enjoys touching herself. She wants to see her daddy's penis. She makes "dirty" sexual jokes, draws pictures . . . and I'm constantly uptight about it. I worry about what she's going to be like as a teenager. I tell myself her behavior is supposed to be normal, but I couldn't talk with my mother about sex the way she does with me. And I could never have behaved toward my dad that way. I guess I feel pretty resentful that she enjoys it so much. I always had a hard time with my sexual feelings; I didn't know how to handle them, but I was too embarrassed to talk with anyone about them.

Or we might actually experience some of our past feelings, especially those related to issues or events that were painful or frightening and therefore were repressed and put away.

One of my patients was a woman who'd experienced increasing amounts of anxiety ever since her first child had been born. Within her home she experienced almost no anxiety, but as soon as she left the house she was rendered virtually incapacitated with fear and anxiety. As I traced her history I found that, as a child, she'd moved eight times between the ages of four and fourteen. Each move had brought a totally new adjustment to a totally new area. She'd managed to survive all that relatively well, but motherhood seemed to bring her past tumbling down around her, and all the old anxieties that she'd kept inside finally emerged to be dealt with.

She'd never been close to her parents during her childhood. Understandably, they had been so busy keeping up with all the moves they scarcely had time to relate to this

child who was increasingly frightened by the upheavals in
her life.

Consequently, she learned to keep those feelings locked
up tightly inside herself. When her child was born, however,
symbolic of the frightened child within her, the cover on the
anxiety and fear became loosened, and her own frightened
child emerged.

Or we might find ourselves treating our own children as we were
dealt with by persons in our original family.

One woman first began to talk to me because of the very
negative feelings she had about her daughter. She was
amazed by the amount of hatred she felt toward this child,
and she was frightened that she might physically abuse the
youngster if she didn't start feeling better about her.

Our sessions revealed that the patient had a very distant
relationship with her mother, who was a cold, rejecting
woman. Perhaps even more significantly, she had an older
sister who was consistently mother's favorite, and who was
given whatever warmth mother had to give. Throughout their
entire growing up period, mother quite openly preferred the
older daughter.

When my patient found herself with an infant daughter, all
the old feelings of hate and resentment, pain and anger
toward the two females in her family converged on the baby
girl. And, in spite of herself, she felt enraged almost
constantly by this new female in her household.

When her husband expressed any warmth toward this
child, she became even more incensed that, once again,
she'd been cheated out of the only available source of love
she had.

And if our parental models have been especially inadequate, we
might be functioning as if we somehow had to make up to our children for all the deficits we experienced as children. This is essentially how supermothers are born—mothers who feel compelled to
do everything perfectly in order to keep their children happy.

A woman in one of my groups was a perfect supermom. She
had three well-dressed, well-groomed children, who had all

63

*kinds of activities that provided them with many of life's
enrichments. She was willing to do anything for these
children to make sure they felt well loved; no task was too
great, no effort too overwhelming, to make sure they were
well adjusted.*

*She literally spent all her energy in working for her
offspring, until she finally ran out of energy and was severely
depressed.*

*Our therapy revealed the frightened lonely child behind
the supermom, the child who desperately wanted someone
to love and care for her and to be concerned for her welfare.*

Supermoms get tired. They get back very little for their superefforts. And they do *not* produce superkids. Rather, their children reflect the kind of superindulgence that's inevitably present when
supermoms go to work to produce superkids. Their superefforts
must ultimately collapse, like putting too much air into a balloon,
until it finally bursts in your face.

We've been in the process of changing the rules of childrearing
over the past twenty-five years. We have shifted almost entirely
away from an authoritarian parental model and have drifted toward
a new life-style in which parent and child roles have become re-
versed, with children in charge while parents act like frightened
children who don't know what to do.

I think this has come about because parents have been so eager
to give their children what they themselves missed. They also gave
their power to their children in order that the kids might not feel
frustration or discomfort. We've become a nation of parents who
don't want their children to suffer any deprivation.

But instead of producing well-adjusted, kindly, benevolent children, we're experiencing the rage and outrage of a generation of
kids that haven't had enough parenting. Our best efforts to reduce
their discomfort have produced a group of kids who have no tolerance for frustration, and who want immediate gratification by whatever means available.

I feel deeply sorry for parents who have sincerely tried to do their
best job of parenting, particularly as these are usually well-meaning
parents who want to give up everything for their offspring. But I feel
equal pain for the kids who received too much freedom without

responsibility, far too early for them to handle it, from parents who didn't want them to lack for anything.

And I feel enraged at the kind of collective craziness that caused so many of us to abdicate our parental role and responsibility in order to make things better for the kids. What we've done by changing roles with our children is to put them into adult roles when they're scarcely out of childhood; we've asked them to do the job on themselves that *we* aren't able to do, for fear they won't like us.

Because we, as adults, have felt so much discomfort and such a lack of loving relationships in our own lives, we've looked toward our children as sources of love. Consequently, we've tried to make them into loving adults who'll give us what we seem desperately to need. We've tried to get our children to love us because our own needs aren't being met. In so doing we've ceased to be parents and instead have become equals with our children, courting their favor and fearing their rejection. This burden is too heavy for children in the process of growing up.

We cannot *make* our children happy, successful, or well adjusted. We cannot *make* their friends like them. We cannot *make* them smarter than they have the potential to be. And *they* cannot make *us* feel better about ourselves.

We can only protect them while they need protecting, and help them grow toward independence. But we can show them directly, by our actions, how we believe people ought to behave toward themselves and toward others.

We have a large investment in our kids, and we feel vulnerable about them. Because they're so important to us their success or failure becomes our measure of success or failure as parents and as people. We form a tremendous identification with them; at times it is even symbiotic. If they feel happy, we feel happy; if they feel distressed, we feel distressed. If only we can get them what they want, perhaps we can have something for ourselves. We stand in fear that the world is judging us in our capacity as parents and that it might find us failing.

We look to our kids to give us those things we feel we don't have. If they love us, maybe we're worth loving; or if they love us, maybe we'll learn to love ourselves a bit more. I think we've also

65

allowed our kids to interfere with our marriages. What we haven't gotten from our spouses we've tried to get from our children as a way of at least getting something.

It is hopeless for us to get our needs met through our children or to live through their achievements or their relationships. All that does is to ensure that our children will have little chance to develop separate relationships, because they are hooked into *our* need systems. They will be caught in a terrible ambivalence: feeling hate for our need to live through them, and pity for our neediness and emptiness. All that does for us, as parents, is to prevent us from working on issues that could help us feel more alive and in touch with ourselves.

All this speaks of the tremendous despair I sense in so many adult lives. We have so few sources of satisfaction that we look desperately to the children to help us feel better. The world we live in is full of tension and anxiety: our marriages may be falling apart; our lives are so transient we don't have time to develop close personal relationships; our families are splintered; our neighborhoods are filled with isolated, separated adults; we're having smaller families, so there's an even greater clinging together for some kind of support that we might all survive as equals.

Somehow we must rescue ourselves and regain our own sense of personal worth before we're all destroyed. This will happen only when we begin to reestablish ourselves as adults in an adult world in which we take responsibility for the care and development of *us* as well as the care and development of *our children,* by becoming good parents to ourselves and to our children.

Part of our difficulty in being mothers is that we probably never experienced quite enough mothering ourselves. But it does little good to chastise our mothers for not loving us enough. We have a choice now as adults (which we never had as children) to go about fulfilling some of our own needs. How can we treat ourselves in a kind and loving fashion, which is what mothering is all about? How can we develop close, loving relationships and do things that make us feel good? What can we do to make the world in which we operate have love and caring in it instead of indifference and hostility?

If we have a mothering deficit and have come to an awareness about it, we now have an option to be a good mother to ourselves in a way that didn't happen before. If we do some good mothering for ourselves, we will grow more tolerant and more understanding of our mothers' inability to give us what we needed. *If we feel we've been mothered already, we're much more prepared to do some mothering ourselves.* If we don't feel we've been mothered sufficiently, we're going to feel anger and resentment for having to give out what we didn't get.

We probably never experienced enough fathering either, and therefore, as women, we may carry around a great uncertainty about our right and our capacity to be assertive, adult women. When we try to be assertive we come on too strongly sometimes because we haven't had sufficient experience in expressing our feelings. Sometimes we don't come on strongly enough, thereby not getting what we want and reinforcing our position that women can't have what they want.

Without sufficient fathering we might find it difficult to be direct and assertive in our relationships with our youngsters, which means we might have trouble hanging on to our parental role. As children move past the nurturing time in their development, they become more assertive themselves. They test and challenge our authority on every possible occasion. It's essentially a growing-up game that children must play with their parents.

But if we don't feel strong in our role as adult parents, we'll be intimidated by our children's challenge. If we falter in the expression of our own rights and responsibilities in the home, children are quick to detect a chink in our armor and to come in even harder with their demands. If it becomes a contest and they begin to win more often than not, we will all have lost.

Children need to test and challenge, but they expect to "lose" most of the time (although they won't admit it), which is to say, they expect their parents will probably say "no" to most of their demands. If this doesn't happen because we've become afraid to say "no" to them for fear we'll lose their affection, then it's quite confusing to children who are programmed to attack and retreat until they're finally free of us. It's like winning the battle before even fighting for it, and that means children grow up never having tested their own strength.

If we don't feel we have the right to be assertive with our families, which is to insist upon getting what we need from life, we'll inevitably be ignored and disregarded by our families, which will only increase our sense of rage and frustration, and make the atmosphere in which we live one of quiet desperation and hopelessness.

I hear constant complaints from women who don't know how to handle their growing children. They're afraid to say "no" to them; they're afraid to deny them anything; they're afraid to frustrate them in any way; they're afraid of damaging their psyches or emerging egos.

Even worse, they are being victimized by their children's demands for more and more. Ultimately, they either strike out in great rage at the injustice of their situation and then feel terrible guilt and remorse, or they simply lie down and become the family door mat, an object of disrespect by all.

If we've had a good parental model of assertive behavior, we can provide the structure our children need to challenge, and perhaps we can even enjoy (at times) the game of challenge-and-check we play with them. But if we haven't had this experience, we're like persons on a roller coaster: plunging up and down, desperately hanging on until the ride is over and our children are grown up. If that's the case, we must relearn how to be assertive ourselves, painful as that might be.

Try to say "no" when your children place demands on your time and life as if these had no importance to you.

Try to insist that your children assume some of the responsibilities you've always taken on yourself.

Try to find activities that help you understand who you are and that allow you some self-expression as an individual, not just as a family member.

Try to understand that your job as a parent is not just to love your children; it's to show them what being an adult is all about. *You can only do that by feeling like one.* Our sense of strength, competency, and power are what make us feel like adults. These feelings are the things we must develop in our children if they're ever to become adults themselves. If we continue to do everything for our children instead of allowing them to learn to do things for themselves, they'll never grow up.

And if we never allow our children the opportunity to deal with the consequences of their actions, we deny them the chance to be adult at all. We cannot protect our children from the realities of life that talk about cause and effect, action and reaction. We help them best by being realistic in our expectations of their behavior and by being consistent in our reactions to their performance.

Having children allows us to become reacquainted with some of our needs *in order that we may now fulfill them.* But it won't happen unless we take the time to be concerned for and about ourselves.

It is necessary for us to recognize our own needs for caring, nurturing, touching, and closeness, as well as our needs to be capable, alive, strong, and independent. And it is necessary for us to act in ways that bring us fulfillment of those needs.

Then *and only then* can we begin to do good parenting for our children. Then *and only then* can we allow them to be children, because *we will have given ourselves permission to be adults.*

I was having a terrible time with my daughter. She had been in and out of trouble for a couple of years—not bad trouble, but defiant, rebellious stuff that made our relationship just awful. I felt trapped, cornered, and totally helpless in the relationship. Each time I would say "no" to something, she would push at me and push at me until I finally gave in. The giving in was always wrong and I knew it. Finally, one day when she was sixteen, I took the chance of saying "no" to something that I knew I had to do. And I stayed firm. She cried and screamed and argued; finally, she became quiet. It changed everything in our relationship and it changed the direction of her life. It was just right, for both of us.

CHAPTER 8
Women and Their Husbands

This final special relationship, in many ways the most significant special relationship we ever deal with, is the one between a woman and her husband.

We enter into this relationship in varying ways. Some women move right into a marriage from the primary home situation. Some work for a while before they get married. Others go to school and then get married. But no one has good, direct preparation for what's essentially her most serious commitment. There are no good training courses for marriage. It's much more a matter of learning by doing, a kind of trial-and-error method for living, an endless series of on-the-job learning situations that occur throughout a marriage's history. No marriage is ever static, and no marriage relationship is ever totally predictable or totally consistent, much as we'd like it to be. Rather, each partner brings her or his entire history into the marriage in hopes that these two histories can somehow converge into one marriage with lasting properties. It's a big job.

Marriage is the place where growing up occurs or doesn't occur. I don't mean the kind of growing up concerned with reaching some mature adjustment to life. Rather, I'm talking about the kind of growing that involves getting current needs filled and old issues settled, and which includes growing *toward* a deeper knowledge of yourself and your partner.

The difficulty is, most people don't know how to *use* the marriage relationship to get something for themselves. They get too involved in feeling guilty about being selfish, or they're guilty about having any needs at all, or they don't think they have the right to make demands on their partners.

As a result, the marriage continually comes up as *useless* and *disappointing:*

My husband and I never communicate.

≈

My husband turns me off. He just hides behind his paper or in front of the television.

≈

All my husband ever wants to do is go to bed with me.

≈

My husband never does anything around the house.

≈

My husband never does anything with the kids. I have all the responsibility.

≈

My husband must think I'm too stupid to know anything. We never have an intelligent conversation when we're alone, but when other people are around he's a brilliant conversationalist.

≈

I do all the work; he has all the fun.

≈

I'm stuck at home, while he's out traveling around to all kinds of interesting places.

≈

Everything revolves around him. If he needs to sleep, we're quiet; if he wants to relax, we do the work. No one pays any attention to my needs.

≈

He gets the promotion, the bonuses, the good times. He's got a secretary to tell him how great he is. I get the dishes, the diapers, the dialogue with the two-year-old, the dirt, and the drudge. It's not fair.

On the other side are the disappointments that he describes.

She doesn't seem to understand how tough it is to make a living and have to go to work everyday. All she has to do is to arrange her tennis and her groups. I really resent all the freedom she has.

≈

I guess I wanted someone to take care of me, to be concerned with what I needed. I find that I'm the handyman around the house and not much more.

≈

She was always interested before. Now I can't get her involved in sex at all.

≈

It was OK until we had children. Now the focus is always on them. The dog gets more stroking from her than I do.

≈

Her liberation scares me. I get very defensive and don't know how to act. If I try to take charge, she gets defiant. If I'm too nice, she gets angry. I can't win.

We have such high hopes for our marriages, and such high expectations. The trouble is, we usually don't let our partners in on these expectations. We don't tell them directly what we need and want from the marriage. We'd much rather they just *knew* what we want and need without having to *tell* them. I think there's a part in all of us that yearns to be "known" just for who we are, without having to tell anyone how to do it; and to be loved, just as we are, without having to ask for it.

But our high hopes and high expectations are doomed to disappointment. For the simple fact is, people don't really know us until we decide to tell them who we are; and they don't always know how to love us the way we need to be loved.

Sometimes we don't even know *ourselves* enough to know what we need, but we wish *someone* would do *something* to make us feel better.

One of the most important tasks a marriage counselor faces is to get in touch with the sense of disappointment and pain that each person feels. At first, each is projecting or externalizing the problem:

If it weren't for his job . . .
She's always complaining . . .
If we had more money . . .

Gradually, the deeper pain emerges: the loss of a dream; the hurt of disappointment; the despair of time wasted and gone.

We get caught in a trap of not wanting to hurt our partners' feelings. And so we don't express our needs; we don't express our disappointments; we don't express the anger and resentment we feel over being disappointed, because that may make our partners feel bad. Instead, we let these feelings accumulate and intensify; ultimately, they explode.

The sequence goes something like this:

I was so in love with him. I just couldn't wait to get married. I knew we were young and that there'd probably be some problems, but I just knew our love was strong enough to carry us through anything.

Followed by:

I just don't know what's wrong. We started out so close, but it seems we never have any time together. Our lives are on separate roads, and we never see each other.

And finally:

I'm sick to death of him and his demands and this house and these kids. I've lost all feelings for him except my angry feelings. I don't want to go to bed with him; I've lost all my sexual feelings toward him; I get rigid every time he comes near me. I don't want him to touch me at all.

Certain issues begin to be the focus of all the anger and disappointment in the relationship. Sex, money, in-laws, the children are all used to divert feelings away from the real issues, which involve a deep sense of disappointment and resentment that this wonderful relationship, for which there were such hopes, hasn't worked out.

Sometimes it takes years before these resentments and disappointments finally emerge in the open. But they've long been expressed in more subtle, socially acceptable ways.

He *is still on a traveling job, when he might be working in
the office.*

≈

She *develops headaches and/or other somatic conditions
every time he wants her to have intercourse.*

≈

He *is engaged in all kinds of community and church affairs
that keep him busy five nights a week.*

≈

She *is busy devoting her life to the children, being a
supermom, which takes up all her time.*

≈

They *never go anywhere alone but always have friends with
them.*

These are devices we use to avoid facing the fact that we're angry our marriages aren't fulfilling our expectations.

Most of us are uncomfortable with our angry feelings. We don't
know how to express them; we don't think they're nice, and we're
quite sure they'll hurt someone, which usually means we'll ultimately get hurt ourselves if we express them. We don't think it's
appropriate to express disappointment about our marriages, because that would mean open acknowledgment of our failure as
marriage partners. And to express resentment would imply that the
persons to whom we are married don't really love us very much,
after all. These are hard feelings to live with.

We've placed such a load of idealism on this institution called
marriage, we've put it in a position that can only produce failure.
We've created an image of marriage in which husbands and wives
live happily ever after. We've created model husbands and model
wives who bear no resemblance to real-life people. And we've
sanctioned and projected a beautiful marriage between two persons
who experience no conflict and no failure in their relationship.
There's a kind of fairy tale, happily-ever-after sense about marriage
that we carry around with us. Most women still look to the men
they marry to be strong, to take good care of them, to be able to
make wise decisions, and to be good providers for their families.

Many people are quite unprepared to deal with the realities of
married life. When a husband turns out to be "real," having a

75

normal range of feelings, he's considered weak and ineffective. When a wife expresses resentment or disappointment, she's categorically a complaining bitch. When either tries to express who he or she really is and what he or she really feels, the world around them starts rumors they're having trouble with their marriage.

We need to take a long look at marriage. We need to be reminded that any close relationship tends to be ambivalent, meaning we experience conflicting sets of feelings about the same person. We also need to recognize that marriage is between two people who've done a great deal of living separately before they came together to live in a common household. That means they carry with them certain joys and accomplishments, as well as certain holes in their development: disappointments, pain, and the coping mechanisms and defenses they've learned to use to avoid their pain and disappointments.

Most of us carry around a lot of unmet needs and pain and we long to have those needs met by someone who will always love us. But we may also defend against having those needs met *because they've been unmet for so long.* In other words, we're hurt and angry at the same time. We want other persons to love us, but we'll almost fight to keep them from doing just that. It's like a kid who desperately wants a piece of candy but gets stuck saying, "No, I can't have it because I don't deserve it," and therefore won't take it.

When we get married we hope these needs will finally get taken care of. *But we dare not directly ask.* Asking would broadcast we weren't as cool, neat, or well put together as we'd like those around us to think. Because we secretly know or fear just that, we guard even more against others knowing it too.

Consequently, the marriage can't be real. Our greatest fear is that, when our partners find out how deep our needs really are, we'll surely be rejected, as we've been rejected in the past, and we'll be all alone with our hurt again.

This is the fear the child within us must guard against. For wanting and needing in marriage is like wanting and needing when we were very young and living with our parents. And as we were afraid to express our negative feelings to our parents for fear they'd get rid of us, we carry forward the same fear and anxiety in relation to our marriage partners. People put up with terrible amounts of pain in a marriage to avoid expressing their deepest needs to be cared about.

One couple I worked with had been married for twenty-five years before they came in for marriage counseling. By this time they spoke only occasionally to each other; they didn't have sex anymore; they spent virtually no time together. Yet, when they were together, they found themselves constantly fighting. Their children had finally grown up and gone, and the buffer their children had placed between them no longer existed. Consequently, they had only each other to deal with.

Both were deeply lonely people, but because they'd spent so much time without love, their needs for love were enormous when they married. The fear of expressing those needs prevented the couple from articulating them to each other.

They had children instead. Both lavished attention on the three children the marriage produced, but neither partner would give anything to the other.

After twenty-five years of this behavior neither was willing to relinquish his or her position. Even when asked to do just one thing for the other each steadfastly refused. They saw counseling as the last step before divorce. Yet, they really didn't want to divorce each other.

The situation described above isn't unusual. We're afraid to express our disappointment when our needs aren't met. We're afraid that if we express such needs, we'll be seen as weak and dependent. Or if we express our disappointment and anger, we'll hurt and alienate our partners, which means we'll get even less than we're getting now. It's a disturbing circle of deception that goes nowhere.

The reality of marriage needs to be discovered. The man you married is human, filled with human emotions. He can feel strong and independent, but he can also feel weak, anxious, dependent, fearful, and sad. If he's like most men, he's been programmed to feel guilty for having those latter feelings, for they're not considered "manly." He'll try to defend himself against them because they're uncomfortable anyway, and particularly difficult to deal with if he isn't "supposed" to have them. He may also think he risks losing your esteem if he's perceived as a feeling or dependent person, which he views as being weak and helpless. He's not invincible, nor superhuman. Like all of us, he struggles with old feelings of being inadequate and unloved, but he has been more successful at burying such emotions.

In fact, the more men are allowed to get in touch with their painful feelings, their fear, their hurt, their emptiness, the more likely they are to be better marriage partners. For it is in getting in touch with their feeling sides that most men are better able to share their tenderness, their warmth, and their caring. As men have had to stand firm, strong, and in control, they could never allow themselves to experience the depth of emotions that existed within them. Instead, they had to put a lid on their so-called "feminine" side, which only made them more inaccessible to those around them. When men are given permission to feel, each of us is given a chance to be who she or he really is and the relationship is given a great deal more to grow on.

Women, too, are filled with all the human emotions, and we struggle with feelings we aren't "supposed" to have but actually do. Although it's been all right for us to be weak and dependent, it's usually been all wrong for us to be assertive and strong, to express our "masculine" side. Yet, only as we are able to experience all our feeling and sensing capacity are we able to be full participants in the intimacy of marriage.

An alive marriage can be our most effective tool for personal growth. It's *the one place where we can explore who we are and what we need, if we'll let that happen.* This is the most important function marriage serves, for it gives us the opportunity to fulfill our two greatest needs:

1. To be close, to experience a sense of sharing and intimacy with another;
2. To be assertive and to express who we are, to experience our own strength and competency.

As children, we found ourselves in situations where our needs weren't met for one reason or another. As married adults, we *now* have a chance to get some of those needs met, in a way society sanctions. Those early needs for touching, for close contact, and for the caring that's expressed physically and pleasurably between two

78

persons who love each other can be legitimately experienced in marriage *if* those individuals allow themselves to *express* those needs and feelings. We never outgrow our need for intimacy (this kind of touching, close, caring contact that may be sexual or non-sexual). But many of us are afraid to experience it. Marriage partners have sex with each other, but it doesn't resemble the need for intimacy that I'm talking about. Most couples are afraid of intimacy because it involves closeness and caring, pleasuring and being pleasured, and this causes most of us a great deal of difficulty.

If we, as young children, were allowed to feel good about ourselves, intimacy is probably not going to be a problem in later life. But if we, as children, weren't able to feel good about ourselves and our bodies, we may be very defensive regarding the closeness and good feelings we weren't allowed to have. When this happens it becomes a battle *against* intimacy that's fought throughout the marriage, unless something or someone breaks the pattern.

One of the ways we avoid intimacy is by letting children become the *focus* of the marriage.

A couple with whom I worked were never alone with each other. They constantly found ways to include at least one, if not all, of their children in every activity. They were constantly involved in one way or another in their children's lives.

Mother, in particular, felt very much as if her main job was to take care of the children's needs. She also felt caught in the middle of a conflict between being with her children and being with her husband. Usually her sense of responsibility to the family won, and so, time with her husband was set aside.

As we worked together, it became clear that these two persons, who were highly independent individuals, had struggled hard to avoid each other for years. They were frightened at the prospect of being alone, anytime, and couldn't imagine even a weekend away without the children.

Another way we avoid intimacy is to keep our lives so busy with activities that we simply never have time to be together. But whenever we place children and activities before the marriage relationship, we diminish the power it has to be a healing force in our lives.

If you feel disappointed and angry because your marriage isn't proceeding as you'd expected it would, it becomes part of your commitment to your partner to get those feelings out in the open where they can be dealt with. As long as they're hidden they carry with them a far greater power to destroy the marriage than when they're finally released and examined. When angry feelings exist but are held in, they prevent loving feelings from being expressed. It's very difficult to behave lovingly when you're also feeling angry, but surprisingly, it's possible to express loving feelings *after* you've expressed your anger.

If there are resentments and disappointments, express them. But be prepared to hear some from the other side. For seldom it's just one partner that's unhappy with the marriage. Perhaps one of the main reasons we don't express some of these feelings is our fear of hearing about our *own* inadequacies from our partners.

Most couples are unprepared for the fact that their capacity to experience intimacy is greatly enhanced by their ability to express the conflicts they feel. It's as if taking the risk of expressing our negative feelings greatly increases the trust we feel. And increasing our trust enables us to be more open. Openness is essential to intimacy.

It's also true that expressing *all* our feelings about the marriage—the loving, good feelings as well as the not-so-loving feelings—is the only way to make the marriage what we want and need it to be.

A "good" marriage is an alive one in which both partners care enough about the relationship to want to maintain it. If there's a conflict in it, it's because both partners have enough of an investment in the marriage to want to fight to get what they want and need from it.

A "good" marriage takes time. There's no substitute for time together. And if the children and other activities are continually programmed into the marriage, without allowing time for the relationship to develop, then wife and husband will miss this marvelous chance to experience each other in all the complexities both bring to the relationship.

There's nothing healthier for a family than a healthy marriage. But we have too long let the marriage somehow get along, while we concentrated on the children. *Now it's time to concentrate on the marriage.* There's absolutely nothing more important for the whole family than the health of the marriage. When the marriage is going well, it means that parents are getting enough of their own needs met to not have to meet those needs through their children. When the marriage is going well, it means that parents are experiencing enough of their own satisfactions and pleasures to function far better as loving, responsible parents.

When the marriage is going well, it means that children observe adults in loving, human interactions with each other, behaving as adults. What better model for children?

Children thrive on their parents' intimacy with each other. It prevents them from becoming hopelessly entangled in situations they can't handle, which means it gets them off the hook of having to deal with their *parents' conflicts* and frees them to deal with their own.

We can use our marriages for the expression and development of us and for the healing that we all need from past and present pain. No one enters a marriage without some unresolved business from the past. Recognizing that we have residual hurts is the first stage of the process. You can always recognize such pain by its intensity and unexpectedness: you find yourself in tears that you can't account for; you are in a rage without reason; fear or anxiety becomes overwhelming and there seems to be no rational cause. These are signs of unresolved feelings from the past that are making themselves felt in the present, in order that we may experience healing.

Sharing those feelings with our partners is the next stage of the process. For many people, this is the hardest part. It is enough to know that I have old pain. It is very difficult to share that with someone that I am close to. They may not hear me; they may not understand; they may reject my feelings. And once again, ghosts of the past operate to remind us of how we once perceived those who were close to us *and* their capacity to care for us.

The third stage of the process is to separate the past from the present; to let go of those persons in the past who were unable to meet our needs; and to allow ourselves to be healed *in the present.* Letting go of hate and anger; releasing hurt and old tears; giving up our need to have our parents finally love and respect us the way we wanted them to: these are the ways we free ourselves from the past

81

and root ourselves in the present. Letting go always allows us to reach *toward* that which is healing and freeing.

When we were first married I moved into the wife/mother role with a vengeance. Just like my mother, I cleaned hard; cooked hard; worked hard. Of course I didn't recognize what I was doing; it just seemed like the only way to do things. Because it was so familiar, it never occurred to me that there might be another way to do things. Then I found myself getting angry with my husband for not doing things the way I wanted them done—for never being the way I wanted him to be. Never mind the things that he was actually doing. The angrier I got, the more he withdrew from me, so I was getting less from him than before. What was happening, of course, was that he was taking on his father's role of being withdrawn and passive in the face of his mother's anger. So we had a marriage going between my mother and his father, and it was awful.

I had to learn to let go of my stubborn streak that said, "If I have to ask, it's not worth it," and I had to learn to ask for what I wanted. I almost always got what I asked for. I also recognized that what I was giving him was rage, not anger. The rage came out of all my past frustrations and fears and had nothing to do with him. He could handle my anger, but he didn't deserve my rage. And I could choose not to dump my rage on him.

The most significant change came when I recognized that what I was actually getting from him, when I could look at it, was far more caring than I had ever received from anyone. It was his brand of caring that he was offering, not something out of my past experience. Caring, for me, had been maintenance caring: food and shelter and not much more. Now I was receiving love and tenderness, warmth and intimacy, but it didn't fit into what I had known and come to expect. And so it was not surprising that I didn't recognize all I had been receiving from him. Then I could give a whole lot easier. And when I could give of myself and could share my awareness of past pain, I received all that I needed to begin to feel whole again.

Now I can actually feel what being married is all about. I had never known before.

CHAPTER 9

On Really Changing

When we get to this point in our struggle to grow up, it's almost as if we stand in front of another brick wall, one that seems particularly hard to climb over. Here we are: we've tried to look at our current feelings; we've tried to be particularly honest in not denying or externalizing what we feel; we've acknowledged our dissatisfactions and our disappointments. We've looked back into our past history, trying to sort out the relationships we held with mother and father; we've acknowledged some of the pain and loneliness we felt as kids. We've examined some of the difficulties we experience in being parents ourselves, particularly as we've tried to adjust to giving to others, when we have so many wants and needs ourselves. And finally, we've looked at our marriages and have become more aware of how little we use the growth capacity a marriage holds.

Yet, there's almost a sense of "So what?" What good does it do to resurrect all this pain and frustration? How is *anything* going to change? It's hard to believe things are going to get better just by complaining about the way they are. Aren't we simply making things worse? Isn't it better just to look at the good things, forget about the bad things, and accept the fact that life isn't very pleasant most of the time?

It's a kind of disappointment philosophy that goes like this: If I don't hope for anything or expect anything, I won't be disappointed when I don't get anything. Or there's a whole series of statements we use to convince ourselves things aren't going to work out or change anyway, and so why bother to try?

I'm too old to change.

≈

You can't teach an old dog new tricks.

≈

The grass is always greener on the other side (so you'd better stay on this side).

≈

I'm set in my ways.

≈

You'll never change him/her (which implies they'll persist in their rotten behavior, no matter what).

There's a kind of last-ditch resistance that stops most of us cold when we think about growth and change. It has three parts:

1. It won't do me a bit of good to look at the way things are. It just makes me feel unhappy, and I don't like feeling unhappy.
2. Everything will get worse if I express to the people around me what I really feel.
3. I don't deserve to have things much better than they are right now.

It's this third part, the undeserving part, that wins out in the end. Most of us are not convinced we deserve much better than we have, and so we might as well content ourselves with our lots in life. This brings us right back to the beginnings of life and the stance we learned to take toward who we were and what we could expect from the world at large.

We started out as total beings, needing to be loved and protected, and capable of loving in return. But if we weren't cared for enough to fill these needs, through whatever circumstances, we carry within us a painful, hurt part that's very childlike in its need for love and affection, closeness and caring. And if these deficiencies in loving and caring persist into other, later relationships (and they frequently seem to), we begin to build defensive structures around these early needs in order to accomplish two functions: first, to shut off the actual pain we feel from our hurts; and second, to ensure that no outside source can get to them to reactivate them.

In addition, we carry within us the same parental model that rejected us, or hurt us, or operated in a way that didn't give us what we needed. And it's this introjected parental model that persists in telling us *today* that we don't deserve anything *because that's what our experience actually was.*

And so we end up with a hurt child inside who's continually being ignored by a disinterested or punitive parent, also inside, and we come to a dead end, a Mexican standoff, in which no action can take place. It's a closed system in which stimulus and response are always the same: the child wants, the parent denies. We can't have anything we want, or at least so we've learned to tell ourselves. As we take over these parental roles toward ourselves, we automatically continue to operate as our parents operated with us. It's the model we experienced; it's the model we lived with for many years; it comes from people who were (and maybe still are) terribly important to us, even though we're now adults ourselves.

In the counseling setting there's always a time when we come to this dead end. It's a kind of end-of-the-world scene, a state of limbo, like a teeter-totter that's perfectly balanced. On one side is all the past: the imperfections, the pain, the joy, the attitudes and beliefs, the structure we built to survive the growing-up process; the child within us who is hurt, angry, defensive, and resentful.

On the other side is the way we are today: the persistent pain, the endless frustrations, the terrible loneliness we sometimes feel, the ache inside as time goes on and *nothing changes;* the persistent efforts we make to say it doesn't make any difference, or that we don't deserve more, or that that's simply the way it is; the belief that if we don't rock the boat, all the bad things will go away or at least they won't hurt us as much.

We find ourselves in the middle of this teeter-totter, trying to keep everything in balance.

But the real difficulty is that all our energy is spent trying to maintain the balance, keeping anything from changing, which allows us very little energy to do anything else.

And nothing *will* happen to change things until we, alone, decide to get off the dead center of the teeter-totter. We're the only ones who can do it. If someone else pushes us off, chances are we'll climb right back on, one way or another.

Most of us don't believe we can choose to get out of this terrible impasse we've operated in most of our lives. We find all kinds of ways and excuses, from the past and from the present, to reinforce our "no possible action" position. And we put up with incredible amounts of pain and frustration because we can't risk leaving our position and seeing that there might be another way to make things better.

When people come to me in my counseling practice, they usually do so because a crisis has occurred, and they're experiencing real pain. But the question almost always raised is this: "Are you [the counselor] going to *make* me change?"

There's implied in this statement the ambivalence all of us feel about changing. We want to and don't want to. We need to and feel we can't. We feel terribly frustrated but equally frightened. If someone else can do it for us, then maybe we'll try. But we'll fight to avoid it, and we won't look at it until things have reached crisis proportions.

My answer to the question that's raised is always the same:

No, I won't make you change. And no, I can't directly help you change; that is, I can't do it for you. But I will be with you in the changing process; I will go with you, step by step. And I will use all the caring and skill I possess to facilitate the process. It now becomes our problem.

Growing up means the capacity to change and the willingness to get what we want and what we need and what will make life better for us. *This ability to get what will make things better for us—this thing we fight so hard against—is what being grown up is all about.* It's the conviction that, in order to be grown up, we must feel grown up, and we must actively pursue that which will help us in the process, whatever that may be.

It's also the awareness that it takes time to grow up, and that each of us has her or his own timetable for growing. And that growth itself is irregular. It's a series of starts and stops, like revving up a car on a cold morning, when it takes a certain number of false starts before the engine turns over and runs smoothly.

86

In the process we may become impatient with the results. It's not happening fast enough; it's not working well enough. We become discouraged because we want to soar, and we've scarcely gotten off the ground. Sometimes we see real progress, but then something else comes along to make us realize we've got a long way to go. Or we think we're past having a certain reaction, and we're jolted by having it again. We think we're "cured," and we're confronted by our "sickness" one more time.

Then there's a tendency to want to junk the whole procedure, to go back to our old, ineffective, familiar ways. It's hard, this business of changing, and it takes a persistence that sometimes we don't feel. When change is closest at hand, we feel the greatest pressure of all.

In psychological language, there's an approach/avoidance mechanism operating whenever we get close to something we really want. In effect, it addresses the fact that we both want and don't want something, and both positions operate at intense rates as we approach our goal. If you want to quit smoking, you'll find yourself wanting a cigarette more frantically than ever. If you want to attend school, you'll find yourself experiencing extra anxiety while going through the admittance procedure. If you want to get a job, you'll find excuses for not looking for one this week, or you'll rationalize why a particular job isn't the right one. The intensity of this approach/avoidance reaction is real. It's the ambivalence we spoke of before: Do I really want to change? No, I can't change. But if I do change, it had better be quick.

If you've finally decided you really want to look at your life, there are two questions that must be raised:

1. What do I want to change? What do I want to have different? What, *in very specific terms*, do I want to have happen to make my life better for me?
2. *What am I willing to give up*, in order to get this change?

It's the second question, the issue of having to give up something, that is most crucial. It means there's a price tag on growth, one which most of us don't want to pay. *And this is the final resistance we face.*

I'm having a rough time with my teenage daughter. I want our relationship to be better. What I'm going to have to give up is my fear of saying "no" to her. I want her to like me, but she's running our lives, and no one's happy. I've got to give up passively taking no stand and begin to be an active parent again.

≈

My husband and I have a rotten marriage. It's getting worse, and nothing seems to help. I've got to give up pretending everything's OK and do something or get out of it. I may have to give up my security.

≈

I feel lonely and excluded from most neighborhood functions. I keep hoping someone will call me, but no one does. I'm going to have to give up waiting and try to initiate some friendships.

≈

I'm angry with my husband, but I don't tell him openly. I find myself punishing him in more subtle ways, like not enjoying sex, or fantasizing about other guys. I'm going to have to give up holding on to my anger so tightly; it gives me a sense of power, but it doesn't make things any better.

One of the most difficult things we must give up is our *deep desire to have someone else do it for us.* In a way it's like giving up childhood and fairy tales and fantasy. It would be so much easier, we tell ourselves, if someone good and strong would come along and make things better.

But if we fall victim to that kind of thinking, we can't grow. For growing up means *us*—acting on *our* behalf—getting what *we* need. It means us respecting us. It means us loving us in a way that allows us to grow and develop.

Perhaps the single most difficult thing that we must give up in the growth process is the control system that we have built over the years to protect us from ourselves and from others. Early in life we erect a defensive structure that allows us to survive the major and minor traumas that are an inevitable part of growing up. We rationalize, intellectualize, deny, repress, sublimate, fantasize, externalize, do anything that works to keep us from *feeling* our fear, anger, and hurt; our vulnerability and our helplessness. As long as we keep defending ourselves from these feelings, we keep others from knowing them and therefore keep them from hurting us.

Much of our energy are spent in the denial of those parts of us that are uncomfortable or painful. The problem is that those parts are still alive and well, even though they are shut off from us. In other words, whatever old fear, pain, or anger persists, unknown and/or unexpressed, drains our energies and keeps us from moving on with our lives and getting what will make us feel better.

If I must spend all my time trying to *not* let you know about the painful parts of me, we will scarcely have time to have a relationship with each other.

The problem of unexpressed pain is very real and frightening to most people. What we are afraid of is that we will become out of control if we let our guard down. We fantasize that our emotions will spill out and never stop; that the hurt which lies within us is so deep and intense it will be unbearable; or that the anger we feel will be so powerful we might hurt someone with it.

The reason such feelings are frightening is that many of them come out of a time when we were very small, and our emotions felt very large indeed. The feelings of children are intense: love is fierce; hate is justified and lawful; hurt is terrible; loneliness is nothingness; emptiness is absolute and without hope.

And so we wall ourselves off from as many of those feelings as possible.

But only when we are ready to let go of our controls and our defenses will we be free of them. Only when we are willing to let go of some of our hurt from the past will we cease to nurse it and thereby keep it inside where it cannot be healed by the present.

Pain released is pain healed; anger shared is anger set free. Emotions that we open up to the light of present-day reality will cease to carry the fear and dread that they carry in the dark inside of us.

In the process of helping ourselves to clear out the emotional cobwebs of the past, we can become especially good parents to ourselves: we can comfort the hurt child within us; we can understand and accept the anger she feels; we can encourage her to experience her sadness; we can pay attention to her fears. We can love her and help her to grow up.

The first time I became aware of tears held in was a surprise. I was at a business meeting that wasn't going right at all. Suddenly, I found myself sobbing; I couldn't stop. These were different tears. They felt like they were coming from the pit of my stomach. And when they were finished, I felt cleansed. I'm not sure why they happened, but it doesn't matter. No one acted as if I were doing something weird. It was OK. And I knew it was important for me.

I learned, on subsequent occasions, that each time I was able to feel the tears which seemed to come from deep within me, I felt freer and more open than I had ever felt. I knew I had reached back in time and had contacted a part of me that needed care and comfort. I could give it to myself by not stuffing those tears back, by not being strong, but by giving myself permission to finally experience them. Not only did I feel closer to myself, but I was closer to everyone around me.

Once we begin to grow and change we'll probably find ourselves changing in various ways, not just one. If I decide to behave more lovingly, it's not just with one person, but with people in general. If I decide to be more honest, I'll probably practice being honest in as many relationships as possible.

One of the side effects of our changing is the impact it has on those around us. I think we frequently underestimate the impact of the change of one family member on the total family constellation. It's like setting up a kind of wave motion, in which the action of one family member sets up a reaction in other members, that may continue in a whole series of reactions. Sometimes they can be pretty volatile.

It's easy to scapegoat in a family, which means it's easy to blame one family member for all family trouble. That's a form of externalizing we've talked about before. If it weren't for the misbehavior of this one particular member, the whole family would be OK. But if this particular family member starts to get better and changes, frequently the family experiences more difficulty than ever, because their scapegoat's no longer available as a funnel for other frustrations. Sometimes we seem to allow one family member to continue to be the object of family frustration, almost unconsciously knowing that if the source of irritation were removed, we'd have nothing to buffer the painful awareness of our loneliness and isolation.

It's the same kind of mechanism that operates in marriage when we blame sex, money, and in-laws for marital trouble, instead of focusing in on the real issues of disappointment and pain.

In a dysfunctional marriage, one that's not going well, one of the partners is usually blamed for all the problems. *Yet, the marriage is held together by this bond of dissatisfaction.* If one of the partners decides to change and grow, the bond is broken, and the real reason for the dysfunctional marriage can emerge. This can be painful, for it usually reveals years of dissatisfaction and separation for *both* partners.

We need to become aware that change produces many reactions. Once we start the process it has an impact on the lives of all who interact with us. If they're used to our being passive and quiet, they may be unprepared to cope with our newfound assertiveness. If they've become accustomed to our anger, they may find it difficult to deal with our loving. If we've always been accepting, without complaining, our new expressions of honesty will be viewed with surprise and perhaps fear and anxiety. What will come next in our new growth as persons? Will we, in our emerging new self, abandon relationships that were tied into our old selves?

This is the deepest fear of those around us when we change: that we'll somehow leave them, as we're leaving behind old patterns of behavior. In ceasing to be what we once were, we'll cease to be available to meet their needs.

In fact, we will *not* be able to meet their needs in the same way as before. If we go about this process of growing up and changing, we'll be more concerned with first meeting *our own needs,* in order that we may be *better able* to meet the needs of those we love.

And when we do just that, the payoff for everyone around us can be incredibly enriching. When we begin to care about ourselves, when we reach down into our history and truly examine our attitudes and behaviors toward ourselves and others, we start a process that may be the most exciting experience we'll ever have. It deepens our awareness, not only of our own actions, but of the actions of others. It increases our sensitivity to our own feelings, as well as to the feelings of others. It enlarges communication, because it allows us to express feelings in a variety of ways. We may find that the nonverbal messages we send are more powerful than the verbal ones, or that the body language we use has an enormous impact on the persons with whom we interact.

It's like a loosening-up process in which our whole body reflects what's happening to us. Many of us spend so much time being uptight, which means tightened up all over, we constantly experience tension in some form. When we begin this process of growth and change, we begin to relax; we begin to let go of feelings and attitudes no longer useful to us. We begin to loosen up our physical and emotional selves so we're more open to ourselves and to others.

When I'm more open to myself, it means I'm deliberately more tuned in to my feeling system, and that I no longer have to constantly monitor everything that's happening (which means letting the "good" feelings out but keeping the "bad" feelings in check). As a bonus, I can almost assume an observer role with myself and enjoy the fact that *I* am an enormously "feeling" person.

Some of the feelings that may emerge, once I lift off my personal censoring device, may be painful, but the emergence of other feelings may be a totally exhilarating experience for me. It's this whole affective side of us that gives us the ability to feel deeply alive and the capacity to experience real closeness and intimacy with others.

When we let go—when we experience ourselves in living detail—then and only then do we begin to discover how incredibly alive we can feel, regardless of where we are.

By letting go and experiencing ourselves I'm really talking about learning all we can about us, and feeling all the feelings that are part of that process, and ceasing to judge all our actions and feelings as unimportant or inadequate, particularly ones we "disapprove of."

The marvelous part of this process is that when we open up ourselves to the world, inevitably we get some of the "good stuff" in that world back, simply because we're receptive and open. When we're uptight we seldom get anything back, because our selves are closed off from the world. It's as if the door is slammed shut against any intrusion from anywhere. As kids, perhaps we learned the world was a painful, disappointing place, and so we closed ourselves off from it and tried to comfort our insides alone, without help or love from others.

But as adults, we can make the conscious decision that we and the world have something to share with each other, and that we and the world have something "good" to offer each other. We can take the chance that perhaps the world isn't entirely the painful place we grew up thinking it was. And we can even make tentative inroads in checking that out with someone else.

For once we *begin to come alive,* and that's what we're talking about, usually we want very much to share that experience with someone else. The excitement of our personal discoveries becomes even more exhilarating when we have someone to share them with.

And growth really occurs when we're able to let others in on it. Sometimes this is done through the helping professions, having a therapist or counselor who functions to share the growth experience. Sometimes this is done through individual friendships, interactions with persons whom we trust enough to share what we're experiencing. It's especially helpful in a marriage when we can share our growth with our partners. And sometimes we can find a group of concerned persons who come together to share their lives and to share their struggles to grow and come alive.

The point is, we need to share ourselves with others while we're growing. The experience of sharing has two distinct purposes:

1. It allows us to take the risk of letting ourselves be known to other persons, which is a way of giving ourselves to other persons.
2. It opens us up to be able to receive something back from those persons.

Once we begin to receive something back from our efforts to be open, we begin to see the world as a place where we *can* get something, a place where people *might* be concerned about us.

And when love is the commodity we pass back and forth between us and special others in the world, we begin to sense what life is all about, and how it could be lived if we could only take the chance of loving.

Loving, caring, nurturing, comforting between persons is what carries us through times when pain and disappointment interfere in our lives. Constrained and tight, we seem to suffer even more when life becomes difficult. But when we're open with our feelings, we're able to share those crises, and somehow they seem more endurable than when we're alone. Being *with others,* sharing our lives with them, is the best antidote to pain that I know.

The process of growth begins with learning to trust and value ourselves, but it has as its end point our ability to value and trust others. *Being able to love another human being, in the sense of valuing and respecting that person and sharing who we are with her or him, is the most sacred and the most significant act we shall ever do.*

Growing up is a long trip, a form of continuing education in how to change. It always begins at a point in time when we're willing to give up old ways and try something new. But it usually takes a long time to get to that new place.

We can facilitate the process in several ways:

1. By learning to care for and about ourselves, and by treating ourselves with respect and kindness, regardless of how we've been taught to behave, *which means not hurting ourselves anymore.*
2. By learning who we are, what we've come from, how we've learned to behave toward ourselves and others, and how we've learned to cope with life.
3. By trusting the validity of our present feelings without applying a yardstick of rights and wrongs to them, *which means to own them as ours.*
4. By relaxing our sense of what we *ought* to do and instead thinking of what we *want* to do.
5. By listening to our inner voice, the one that first expresses some restlessness and need for change, or that talks about the things we might dare to dream about doing.
6. By observing how we behave and what we do to *prevent* ourselves from changing.
7. By becoming convinced we have the right to change and the responsibility to do something about a situation or a relationship that's damaging or inimical to us, *out of respect and regard for ourselves.*

94

8. By looking for creative options and possibilities that might make a difference in our lives.
9. *By acting in a new way,* taking the risk that must occur if anything is to change.
10. By analyzing the results of our actions, retaining those actions that help us change and grow, and eliminating those that aren't growth producing.
11. *By sharing the whole process,* at whatever stage, with someone whom we trust and care about.
12. *By receiving back* from that person, or persons, care, concern, and support for where we are and what we're trying to do, as well as constructive help in the process.

We hear a lot about fulfillment these days and about various ways we can feel fulfilled. But it's very hard sometimes to know just what fulfillment is all about. Only when we change the word around does it become clearer in meaning. *Fulfilled,* when separated out, means *filled-full.* When we're filled-full we begin to know what fulfillment's all about. When we're filled-full we have something to give. When we're filled-full we know what being a grown-up female is all about.

We get filled full when we begin to care about who we are and what we want from life. We get filled full when we challenge the old voice that says we don't deserve to get something for us. We *are* filled full when we experience what loving is all about.

At the bottom of this process of growing up female is the search for loving relationships that are alive and satisfying, and for an increasing sense of our own worth and independence. We've become grown up *when we assume responsibility for the search.*

Then shall we no longer be afraid of who we are but instead fill ourselves full: full of life, full of excitement, full of the things that make us feel good; full of the richness of closeness; full of the power of knowing our own strength; full of the sense of our own value and our own uniqueness; full of the understanding of who we are and where we've come from; *full of the incredible gift of life.*

And then shall we be able to openly share our fullness with others, that we might know what it feels like to be *grown up—unabridged—and free.*

95

CHAPTER 10

The Unabridged Broad

The term broad, when used to describe a woman, has always carried with it pejorative meanings. A broad is a stupid woman who is good only for sexual intercourse and for pleasing men. Typically, the term appears with the word dumb, so a "broad" is really a "dumb broad." As such, it speaks of a highly limited and restricted individual.

The chapter title "The Unabridged Broad" was chosen consciously to indicate that the real function and role of woman has changed dramatically. There has always been another meaning for the word broad that implies breadth and grandeur of scope, as in broad horizons and broad vision. These are meanings equally and more accurately connected to the word broad.

Therefore the name "The Unabridged Woman" or "The Unabridged Broad" becomes a mark of pride, denoting a woman who is not limited by the stereotypes of the past and who is free to discover her own uniqueness as she adds breadth and possibility to the world in which she moves.

The unabridged woman is a female in process. She's growing; she's changing; she's trying to discover who she is and what she wants to be.

The effort is hard. Sometimes she makes progress; sometimes she seems to slip backward; sometimes she doesn't move forward for a long time. But she continues to struggle to find her own way.

97

She's increasingly willing to own her own feelings, rather than blame someone else for how she feels. She's increasingly trying to express those feelings, whether they're happy and excited, or whether they reflect the sadness and emptiness she sometimes feels.

She's learning she can be both dependent and independent, assertive and passive, without diminishing herself in any way.

She's finding that the more open she is with her feelings, the more comfortable people are around her. She's discovering she can express anger without the world coming apart. And that whenever she *expresses* loving feelings, and really means them, she *experiences* loving responses in return.

She's found that being grown up means being who she is right now: with her weaknesses and her strengths; her successes and her failures; her capacity to cope alone and her willingness to ask for help when she needs it.

She's learned that what she's *supposed* to be may be quite different from what she feels she *wants* to be. And so she's trying not to be governed by *shoulds* and *oughts,* but rather by what she *needs* and *wants.*

She's determined to come to know herself so that she might get those things which will help to make her life filled-full.

She's found she needs to be assertive and direct if she's going to get what she needs.

But she also knows that her needs for intimacy and closeness, when filled, make her feel incredibly alive.

She's learned that the greatest deterrent to her changing is *her own resistance* to growing and getting better.

She knows that her capacity to love and value herself only increases her ability to love and value others.

She knows that in loving relationships she experiences a sense of wholeness and completion which is utterly unique and special.

She's deeply grateful for those special relationships that allow her to be herself: alive, warm, loving, and free.

She's learning to love life in all its incredibleness and to feel deeply a part of all the world around her.

She knows that just in *being,* in being who she is, she comes close to *knowing* all there is to know.

She's been freed *toward* what she *chooses* to be, out of her own sense of freedom and uniqueness. She's not restricted to any one model of behavior, but rather moves among the many roles she assumes, as she discovers her own life-style.

And she would tell you that all of life is encapsulated in one word: Loving.

Loving free, loving openly, loving fully . . .

Loving those whom we've been given to love . . .

And Loving the life that we've been given to live.

CHAPTER 11

On Loving

Finally, in the act of loving we know what life and liberation are all about. We begin with us, in the knowing and caring about who we are. But it is that which moves us *toward others* that allows us to be fully human, whole and healed.

It is not enough that I know myself if I do not share that knowing with you. It is not enough that I love myself without caring about what happens to you. It is not enough that we become adjusted, or mentally healthy or mature, if that does not include an active concern for those around us. Women and men, both, do not survive in isolation.

As our world becomes more complex we increasingly need to be involved in caring relationships that help us to express our need to care and to be cared about, and to overcome that sense of separateness and loneliness which is the most significant human problem of our time.

We begin this life as creatures with an enormous capacity for love, but for many the potential to be loving is stunted or stopped by circumstances that don't allow it to become fully developed. And so one of our most profound problems is to be willing to open up our loving side and to risk it once again. As children, our expressions of love may have been ignored or misunderstood. As adolescents, such expressions were often overwhelming and frightening, full of the intensity of our sexuality and the fear of rejection.

We learn to play it cool and not to let people know how much we do care, or how vulnerable we feel when we try to express our loving side.

And because so many others have also learned to play it cool, we are a people who are afraid to reach out to one another; to come in touching contact; to feel how good it is to be close.

We hold back; we are polite; we shake hands when we would like to hug; we smile when we feel like crying. We get quiet or change the subject rather than express how we feel. We make jokes to cover how hurt or how lonely we are.

We want to reach out and touch and be comforting, but we stop because someone might think it's a sexual advance. We try to appear as if everything were OK or that we have all situations well in hand; when what we want is to have someone hold us or let us know in some reassuring, nonverbal way that he or she understands.

It's that scared, rejected, constrained part of us that holds us back from actively loving. We say, "Love *me first,* and then I'll love you back." Or sometimes we say; "What would people think?"

And so we miss those marvelous chances to touch a hand; put an arm around a shoulder; hold in our arms another human being who, like us, needs to be cared about and to care. We miss the chance to feel the incredible closeness and warmth of a hug that says a thousand words of love and hope and encouragement.

Afraid and lonely ourselves, we hold back from doing the one thing that will free us from our isolation.

Loving is our only way of finally breaking out of the strictures that *we* have imposed on ourselves. But it is only *active* loving that frees us. If we wait around hoping that someone will love us first, or that someone will have to make us feel better first, then we are doomed to reside forever in our same hopeless, helpless place, bound and gagged by our own passivity.

In truth, loving heals the lover more than it helps those that are loved. It is that paradoxical quality of life that says, whenever we reach out and touch another, we feel touched ourselves. Whenever we try to understand another, we learn more about ourselves. Whenever we actively love another person, we experience the strength and warmth and peace that such contact brings.

102

This is the primary and most marvelous miracle of adulthood. *Finally*, we can let ourselves go and feel the power and the strength of our loving self. We no longer have to pretend that we don't care. We no longer have to play it safe. We are no longer threatened by rejection.

For loving allows us to *be* in the fullest and best sense of what *being* is all about.

The words:

I am concerned

I care

I love

are the most important and profound words that we, as human beings, will ever share.

For they link us to each other;

They allow us to overcome our pain;

Finally, they set us free.